The Great Piano W...
LUDWIG van BEETHOVEN

WARNER BROS. PUBLICATIONS - THE GLOBAL LEADER IN PRINT
USA: 15800 NW 48th Avenue, Miami, FL 33014

WARNER/CHAPPELL MUSIC

CANADA: 40 SHEPPARD AVE. WEST, SUITE 800
TORONTO, ONTARIO, M2N 6K9
SCANDINAVIA: P.O. BOX 533, VENDEVAGEN 85 B
S-182 15, DANDERYD, SWEDEN
AUSTRALIA: P.O. BOX 353
3 TALAVERA ROAD, NORTH RYDE N.S.W. 2113

NUOVA CARISCH

ITALY: VIA CAMPANIA, 12
20098 S. GIULIANO MILANESE (MI)
ZONA INDUSTRIALE SESTO ULTERIANO
SPAIN: MAGALLANES, 25
28015 MADRID
FRANCE: 20, RUE DE LA VILLE-L'EVEQUE, 75008 PARIS

INTERNATIONAL MUSIC PUBLICATIONS LIMITED

ENGLAND: GRIFFIN HOUSE,
161 HAMMERSMITH ROAD, LONDON W6 8BS
GERMANY: MARSTALLSTR. 8, D-80539 MUNCHEN
DENMARK: DANMUSIK, VOGNMAGERGADE 7
DK 1120 KOBENHAVNK

Project Manager: Dale Tucker
Design: Michael Ramsay

© 1997 BELWIN-MILLS PUBLISHING CORP. (ASCAP)
All Rights Administered by WARNER BROS. PUBLICATIONS U.S. INC.
International Copyright Secured   Made in U.S.A.   All Rights Reserved

LUDWIG van BEETHOVEN
Born: December 16, 1770-Bonn, Germany
Died: March 26, 1827-Vienna, Austria

Born in Bonn, Germany on December 15 or 16, 1770, Ludwig van Beethoven was a member of a musical family which spanned three generations. His early training, by his father, was on piano and violin, and at the age of eight he began his study of theory and keyboard with the local court organist. Academically, Beethoven was educated only through elementary school, a fate which followed him through his career. His first published work, a set of variations on a march by E.C. Dressler, was in 1783, and more significant works followed shortly thereafter. In 1784 Beethoven took an organist position which afforded him continued musical study and the opportunity to travel. The death of Beethoven's mother in 1787 is seen as the beginning of his financial and health problems. He stayed in Bonn for several years, and by performing with orchestras of the court, gained further compositional skills. By this time he had established a large group of wealthy friends, and was respected by many composers.

In 1792 Beethoven moved to Vienna, Austria, where he remained the rest of his life, to study with Haydn, Albrechtsberger and Salieri. He quickly established himself as a virtuoso pianist and composer, and made his first public appearance as a soloist in 1795, performing one of his concertos. The mid-1790's afforded Beethoven other concert opportunities, including his first concert tour. Although first thought of as primarily a piano composer, with his traditional Classical style sonatas and symphonies, Beethoven led the way in the development of both by building on various themes, adding sections, transitional material, longer introductions, and the use of a fourth movement, thus proving his ability as a composer of large scale works. By the early 1800's he was being contacted by numerous publishers who wanted to print his works.

The early 1800's also saw the beginning of Beethoven's loss of hearing, complicated by recurring ill-health, financial problems, and personal problems with family members. He often fought depression with increased compositional output, and a period of large scale works for keyboard and orchestra were produced between 1806 and 1808. The peak of his compositional career is thought to be 1814, when audiences were large and receptive at his concerts, and compliments were abundant from royalty, which led to the end of his financial trouble. More large scale works appeared in the period beginning around 1817, including the *Diabelli Variations*, considered the ultimate of this compositional style. The Philharmonic Society of London requested two symphonies from Beethoven, a project about which he took his time, but from which came the famous *Ninth Symphony* and its concluding choral movement. During his last few years, Beethoven wrote only for the string quartet. Works from his late period more resemble the Romantic period than the Classical, and were the basis for the development of the former by composers who followed.

Beethoven received a great outpouring of support from music societies, colleagues and publishers during his final days. Following his death, on March 26, 1827, and funeral which was attended by over 10,000 people, postage stamps were issued in his memory in Europe, and streets were named for him in several countries.

The musical output of Beethoven was enormous, including nearly sixty works for orchestra and band, eighty chamber works, eighteen extended choral works, over one hundred vocal works, along with thirty-two piano sonatas, twenty sets of variations, and more than fifty other individual piano compositions.

CONTENTS

Sonatina No. 1 4
Sonatina No. 2 8
Sonatina No. 3 14
Sonatina No. 4 24
Sonatina No. 5 26
Sonatina No. 6 28
Contra Dance No. 1 31
Contra Dance No. 2 36
Contra Dance No. 3 38
Ecossaise 42
German Dance No. 1 48
German Dance No. 2 52
German Dance No. 3 56
Sonata, Opus 2 (second movement) 62
Sonata, Opus 7 (third movement) 64
Sonata, Opus 10, No. 2 (second movement) 66
Sonata, Opus 10, No. 3 (third movement) 70
Sonata, Opus 13 "Pathetique" (complete) 72
Sonata, Opus 27, No. 2 "Moonlight" (complete) 88
Sonata, Opus 28 (third movement) 105
Sonata, Opus 49, No. 1 (complete) 107
Sonata, Opus 49, No. 2 (complete) 115
Rondo, Opus 51, No. 1 123
Bagatelles
  Opus 33, No. 2 130
  Opus 33, No. 3 134
  Opus 33, No. 6 136
  Opus 33, No. 7 137
  Opus 119, No. 1 140
  Opus 119, No. 5 142
  Opus 119, No. 8 143
  Opus 119, No. 9 143
  Opus 126, No. 2 144
Rondo a Capriccio, Opus 129 146
Polonaise, Opus 89 156
Nine Variations on a March by Dressler 163
Six Easy Variations on a Swiss Song 170
Six Variations, Opus 76 172
Seven Variations on "God Save the King" 176
Selected "Diabelli Variations," Opus 120 182

SONATINA NO. 1
in E flat Major
I

LUDWIG van BEETHOVEN

5

6

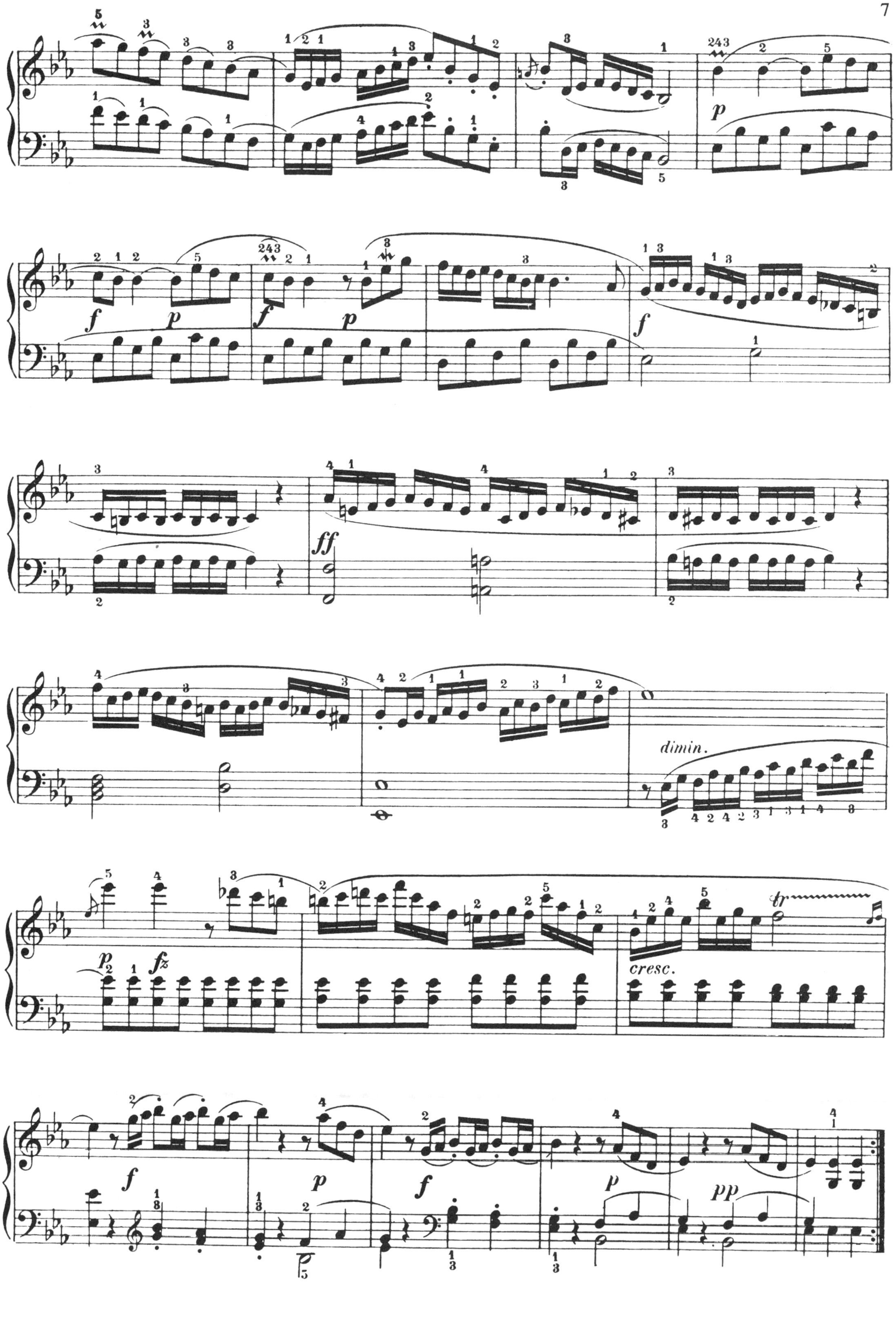
p
f
p
f
p
f
ff
dimin.
p
fz
cresc.
tr
f
p
f
p
pp

SONATINA NO. 2
in F Major
I

Larghetto maestoso

9

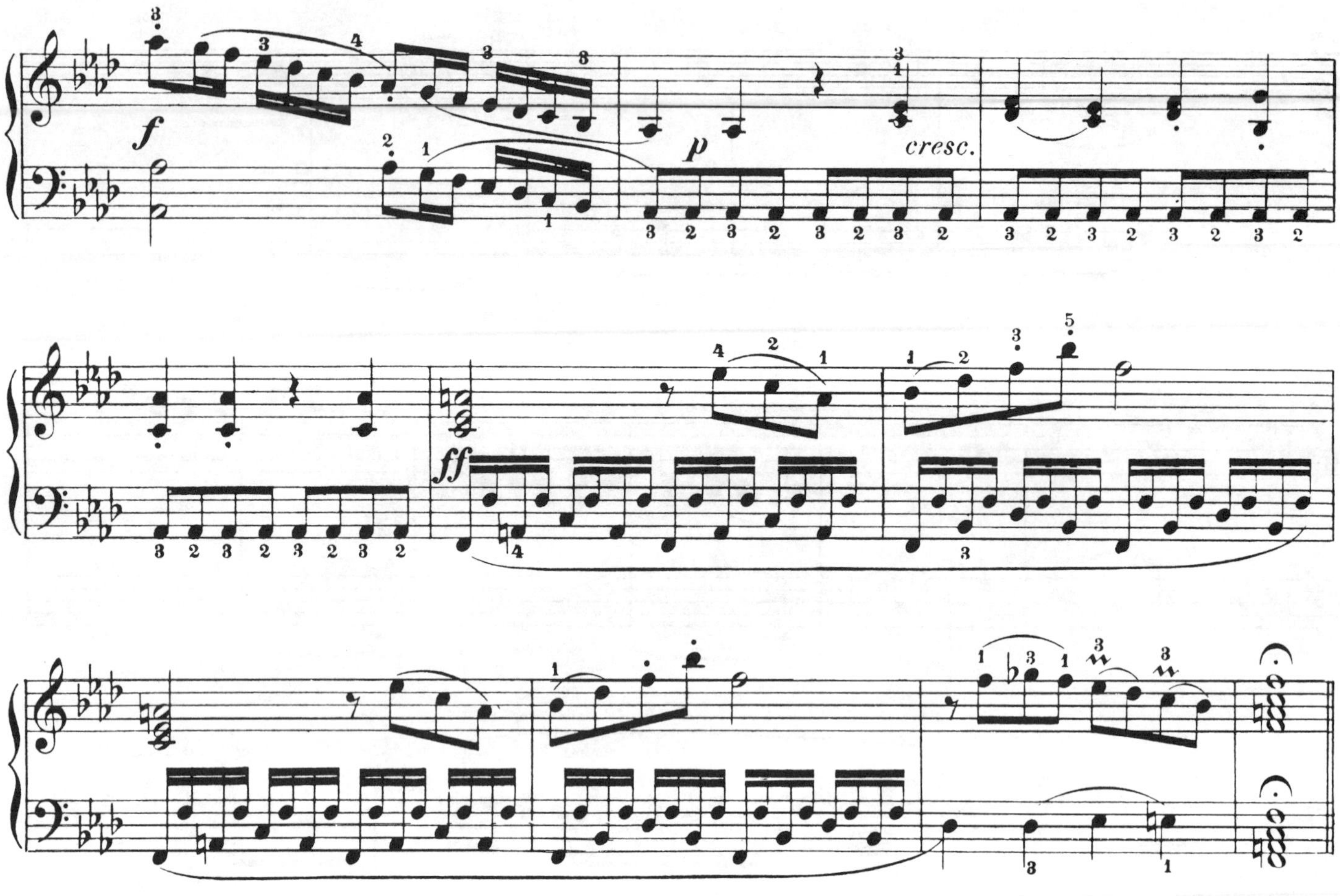

Larghetto maestoso

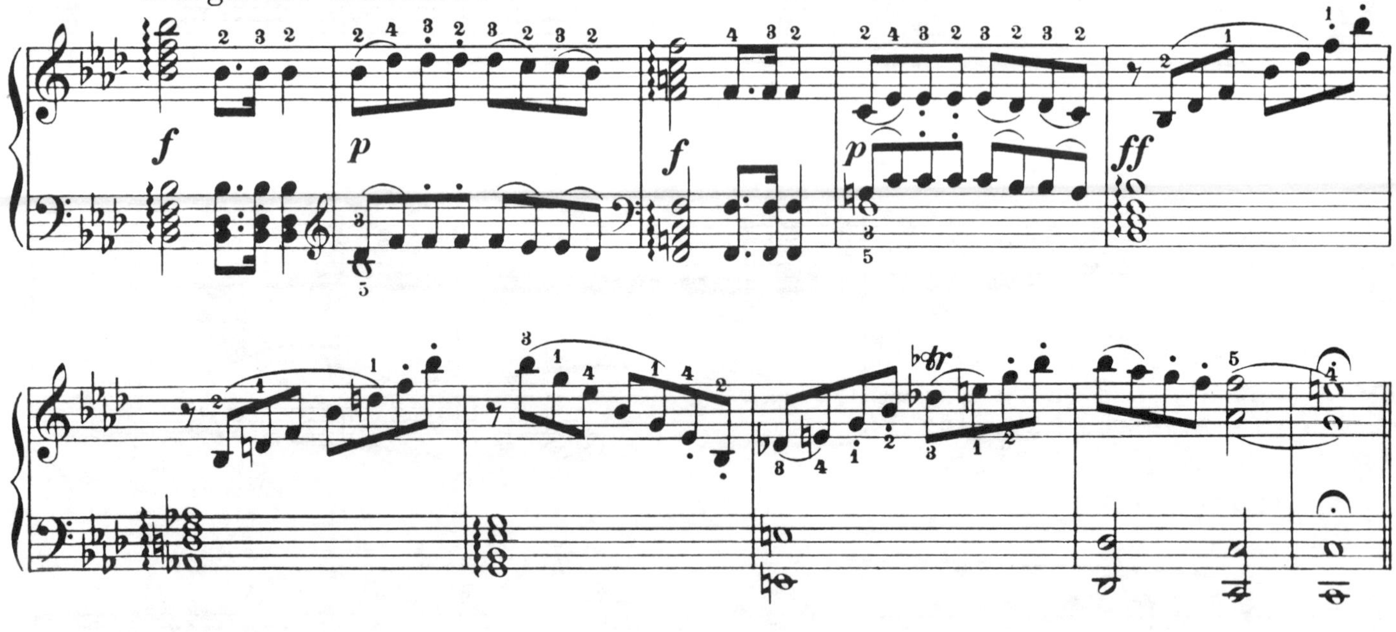

Allegro assai

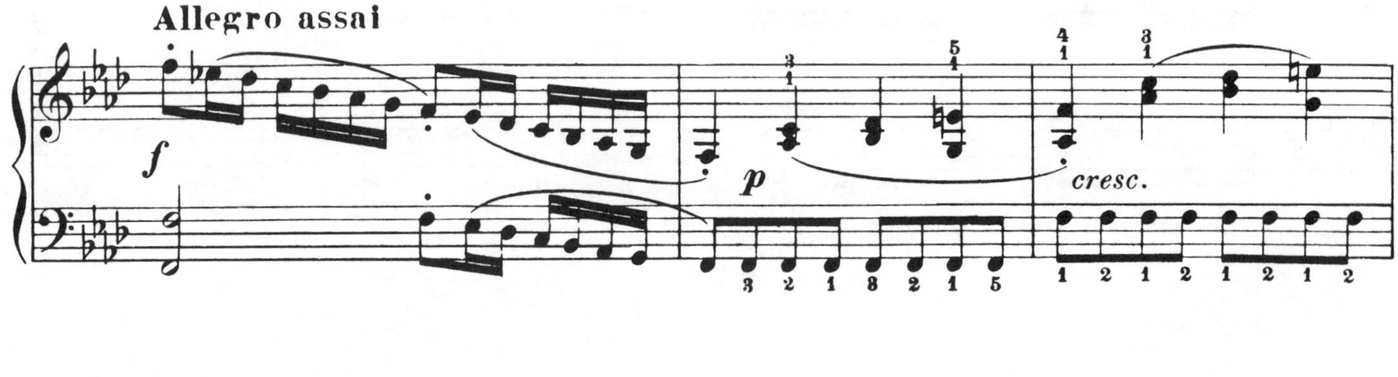

11

III

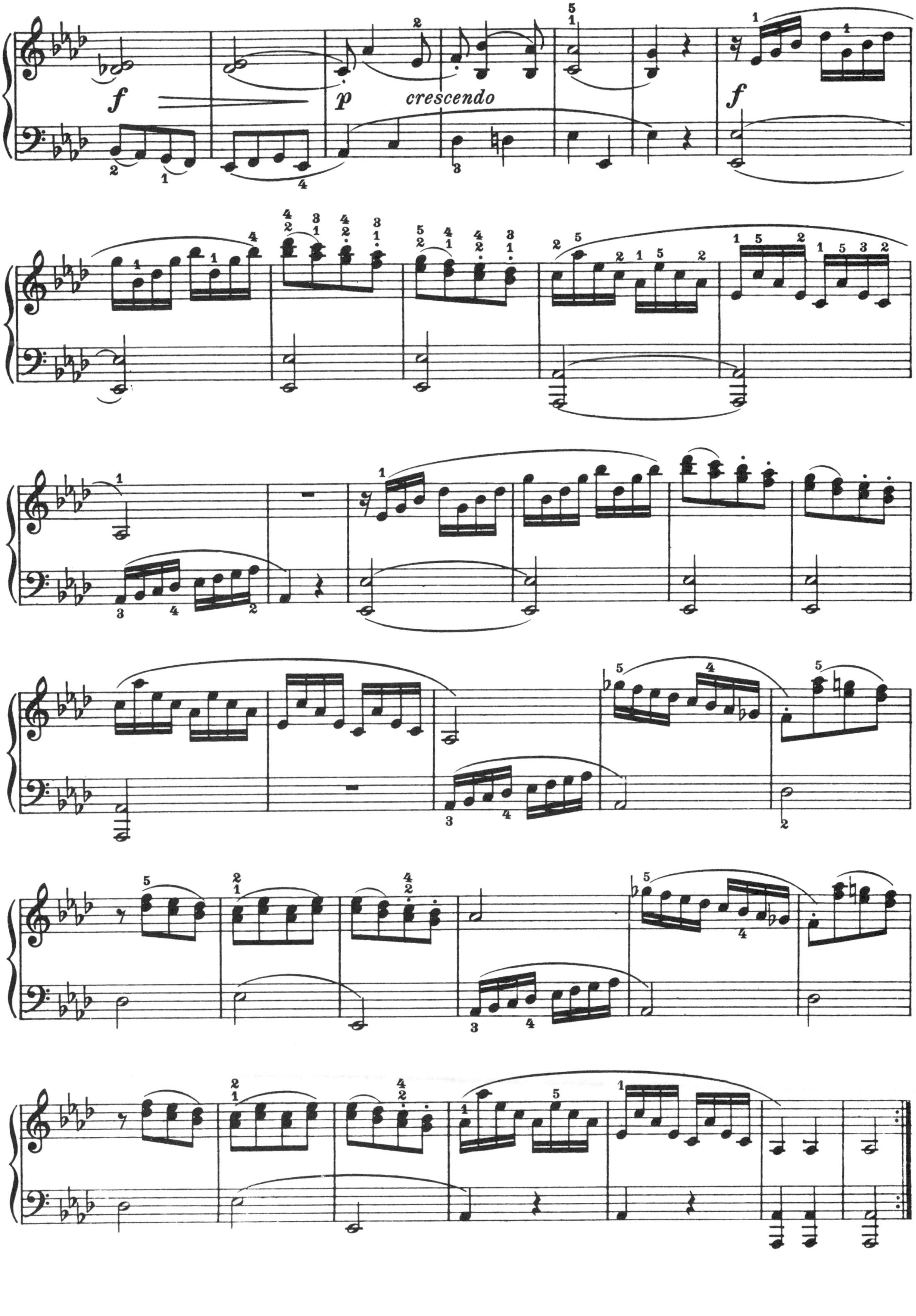
f
p
crescendo
f

SONATINA NO. 3
in D Major
I

Allegro

15

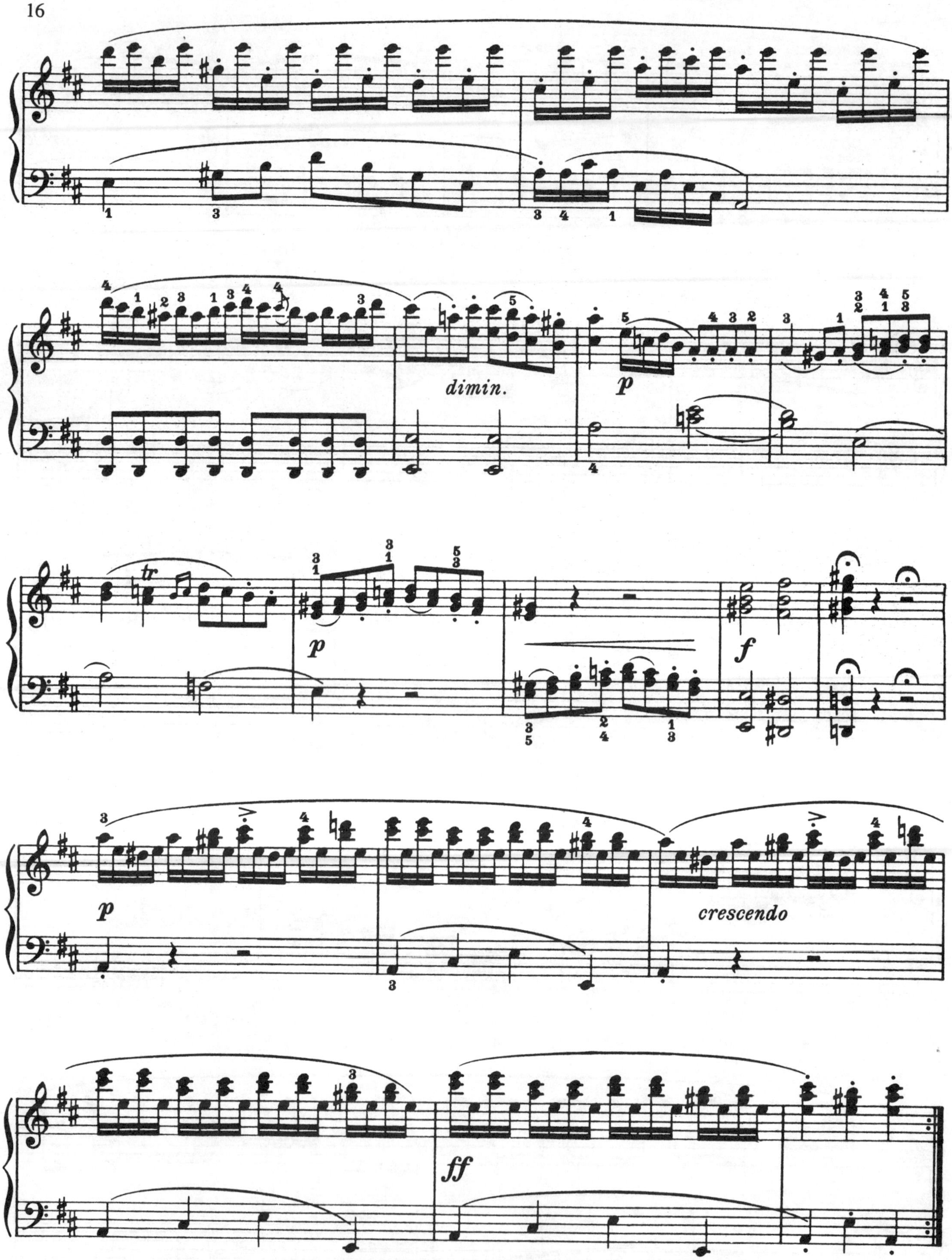
dimin.
p
tr
p
f
p
crescendo
ff

17

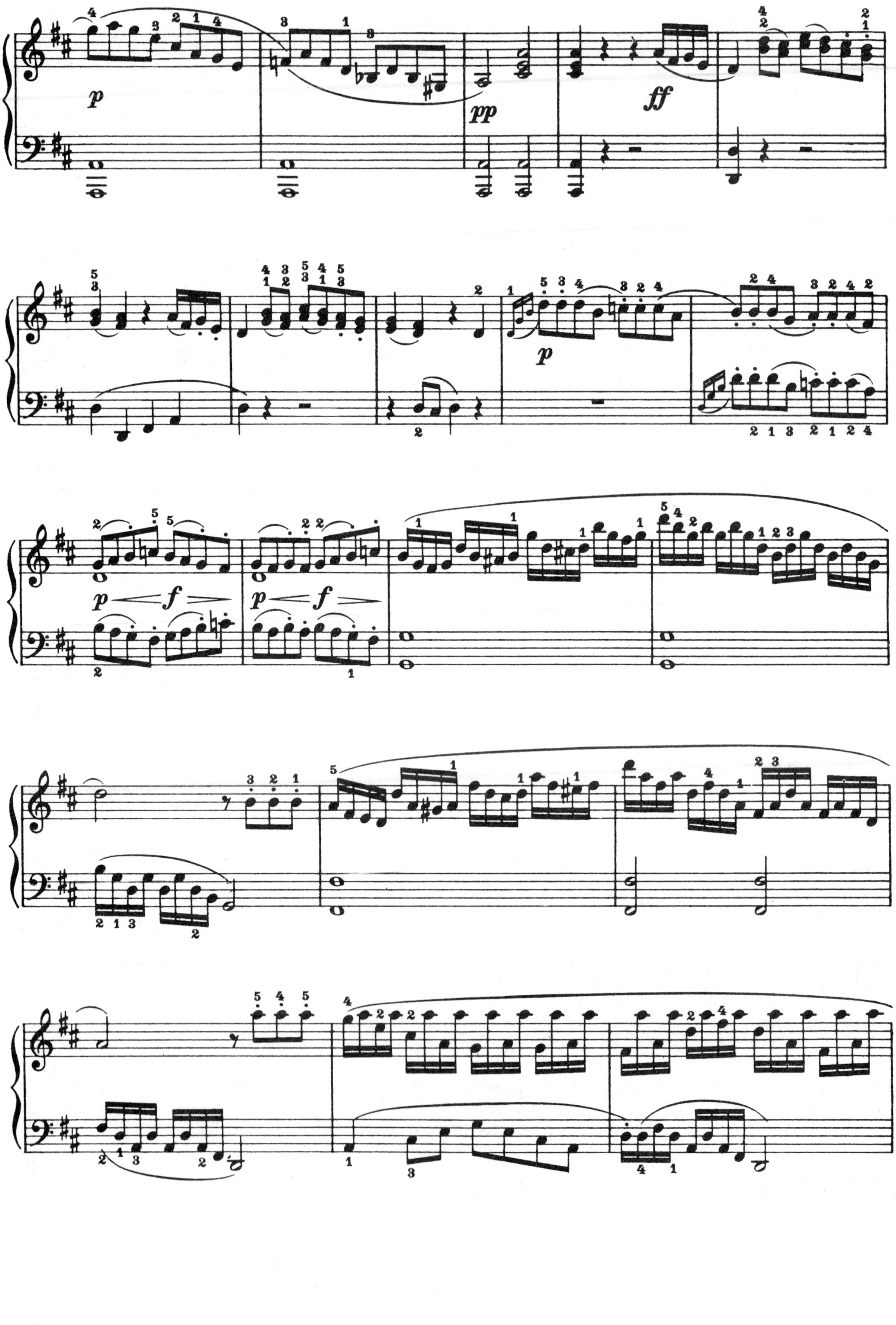
p
pp
ff
p
p f
p f

19

III

Scherzando
Allegro, ma non troppo

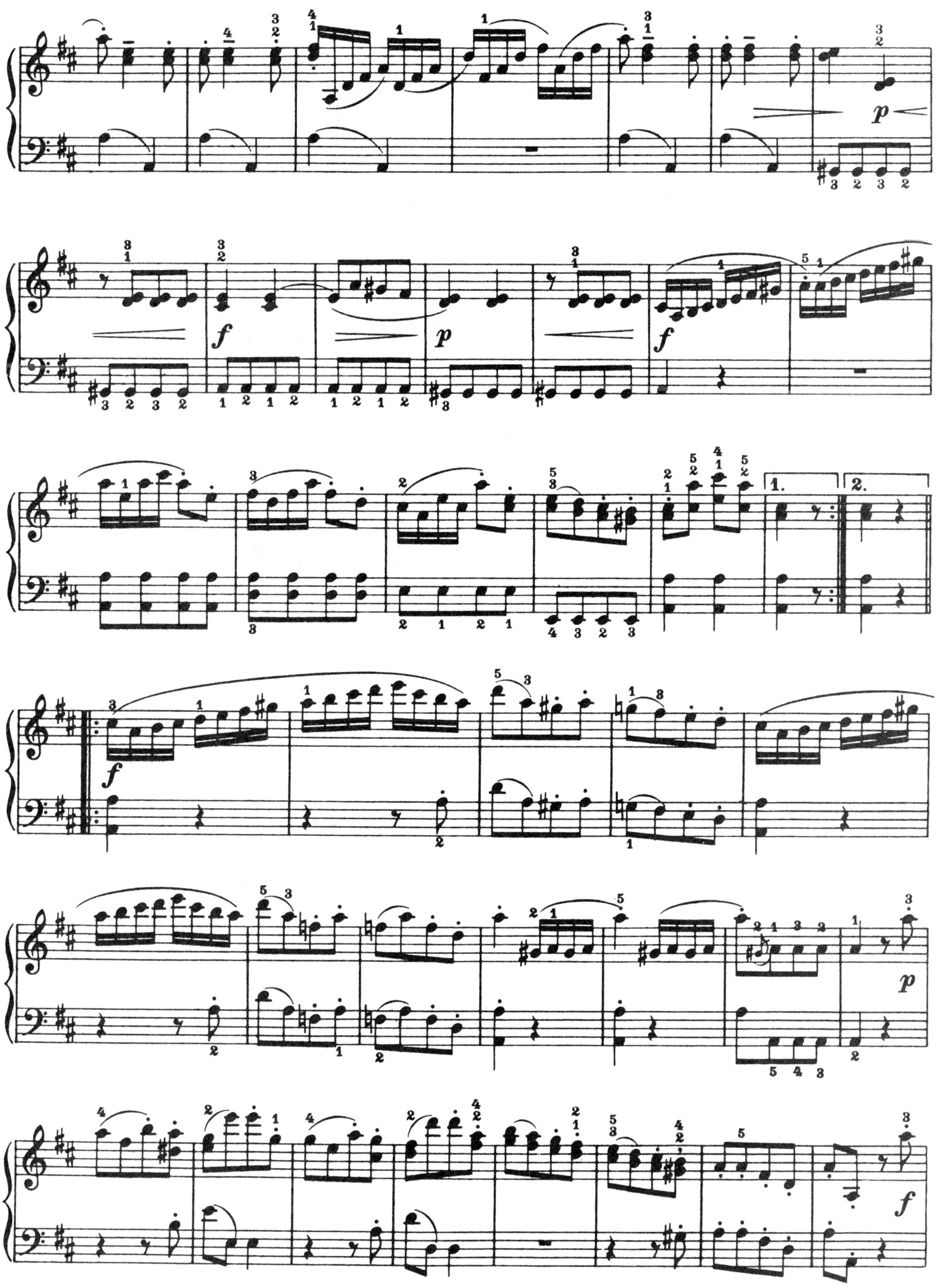

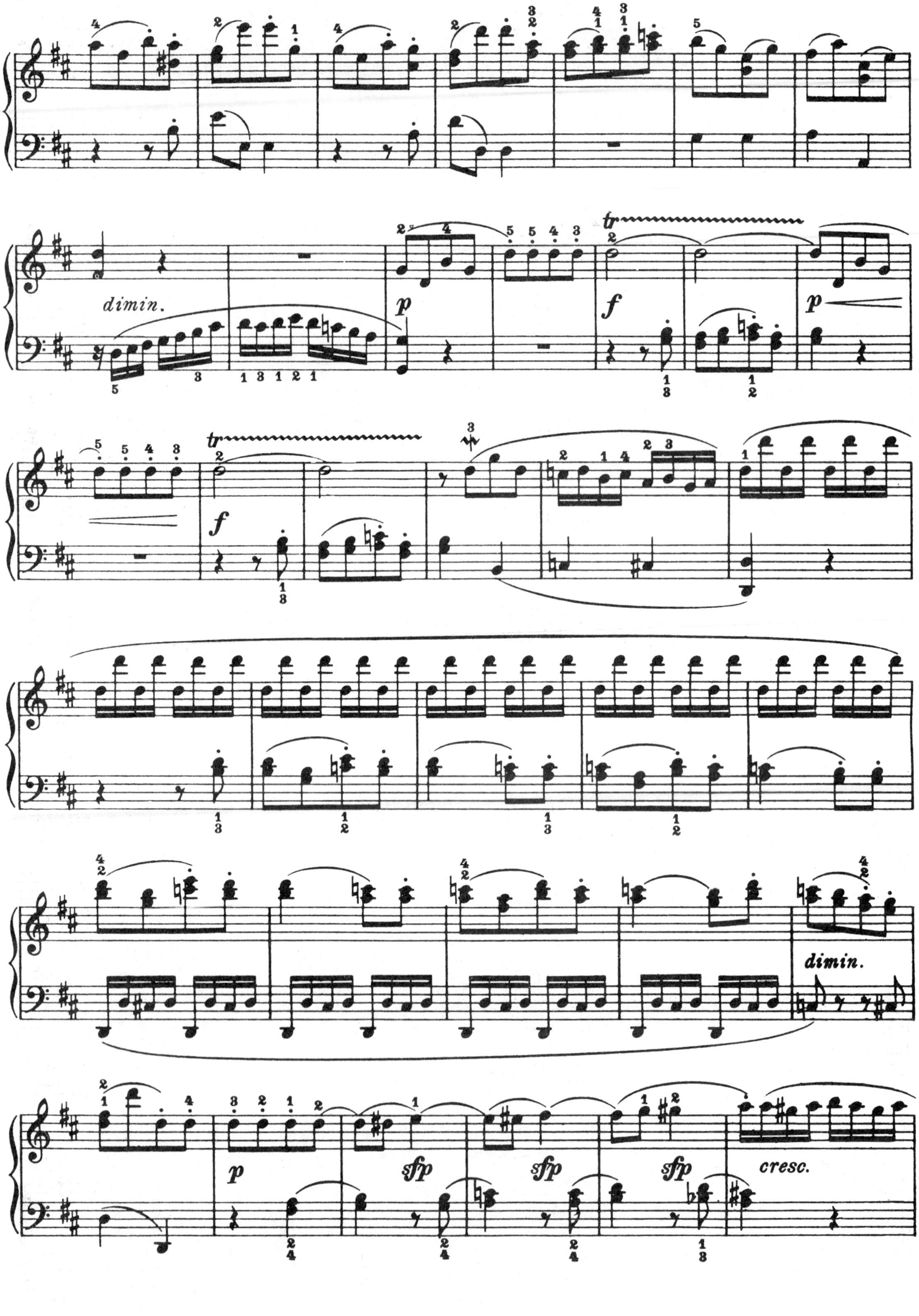
dimin.
p
f
p
tr
f
tr
dimin.
p
sfp
sfp
sfp
cresc.

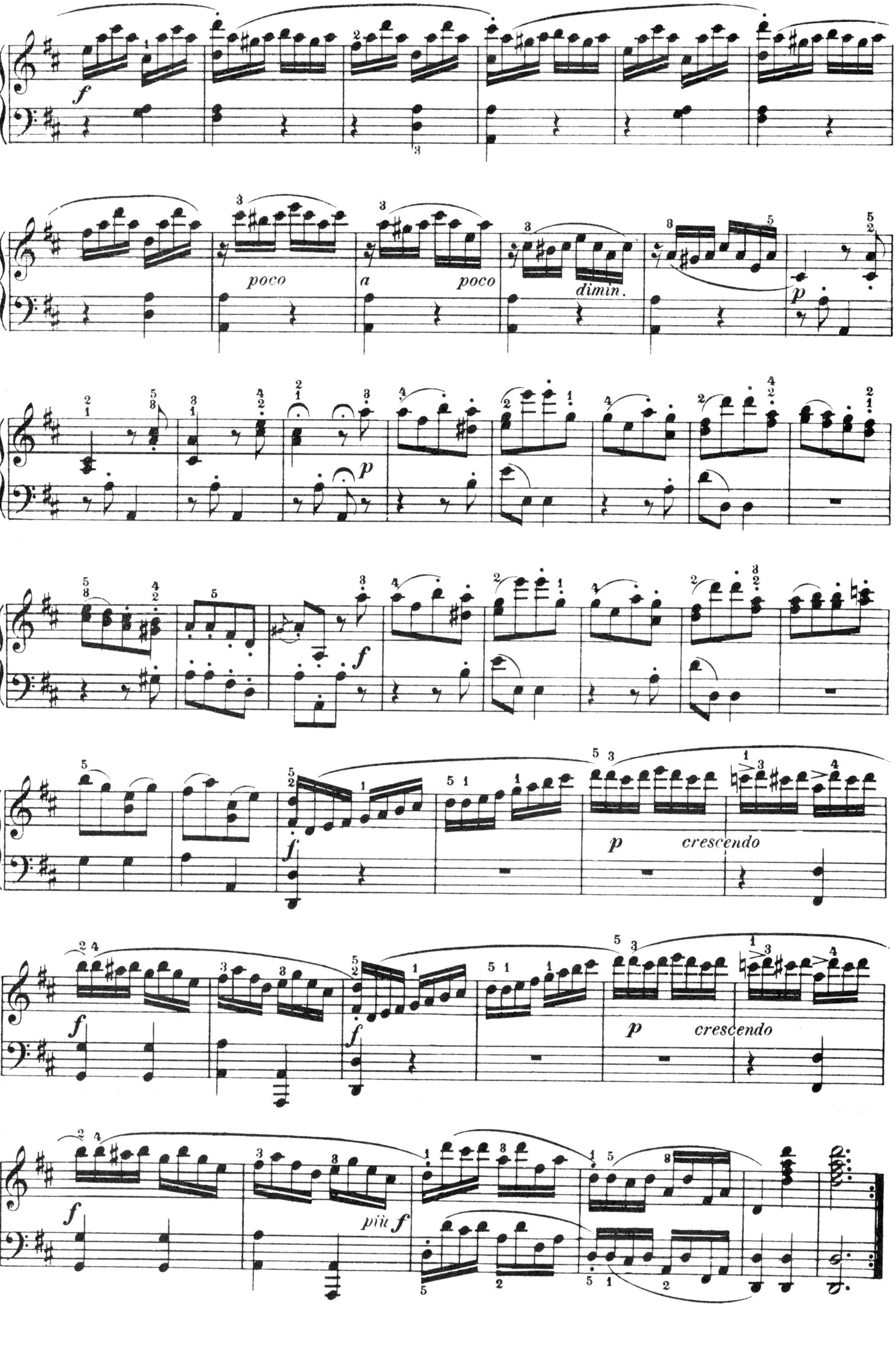
poco
a
poco
dimin.
crescendo
crescendo
più f

SONATINA NO. 4
in C Major

Adagio

II

25

SONATINA NO. 5
in G Major

Moderato

II

Romanze

SONATINA NO. 6
in F Major

Allegro assai

29

crescendo
dim.
dim.
poco marcato
crescendo
cresc.
ad libitum
a tempo
dimin.

CONTRA DANCE
I

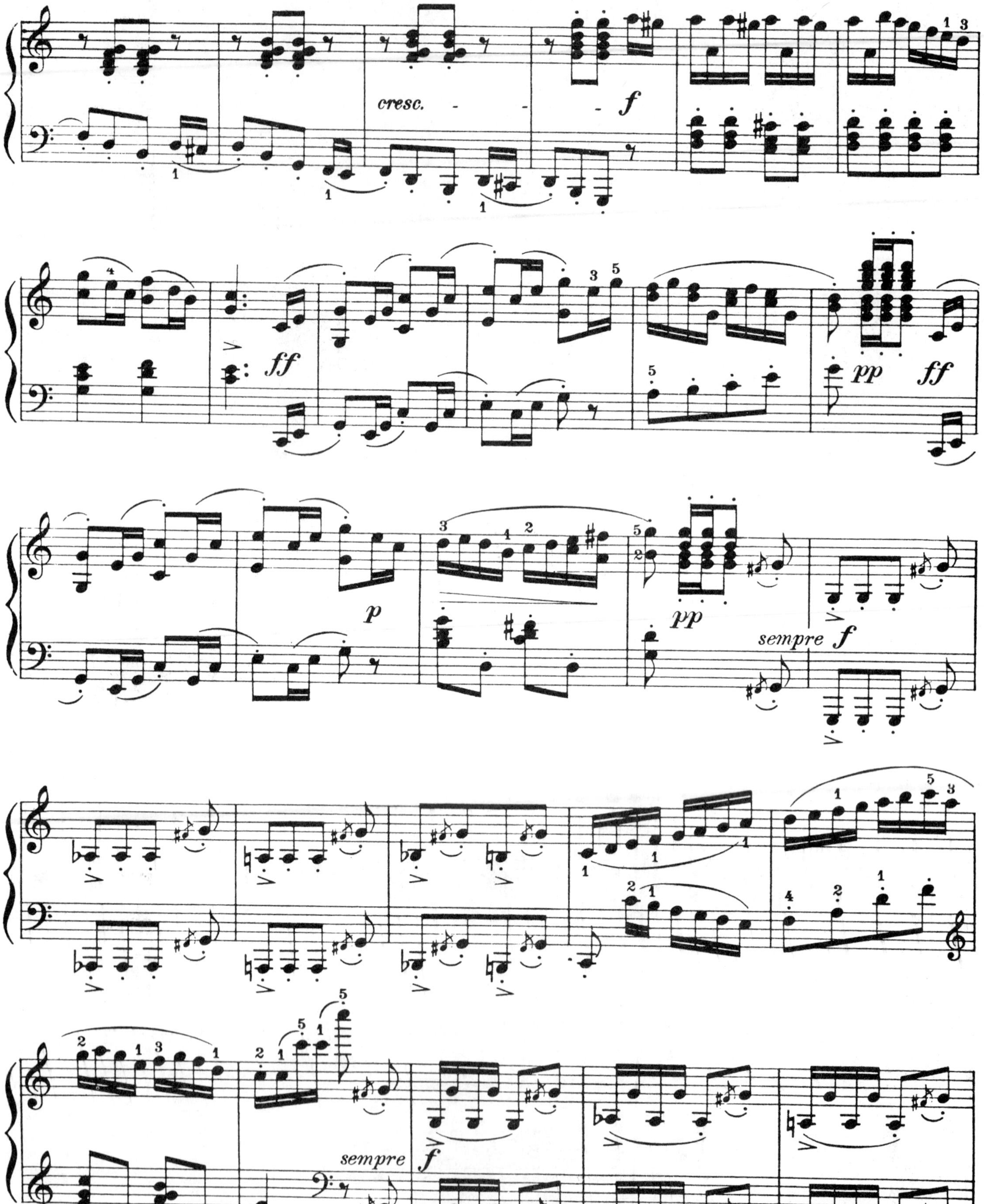
cresc.
f
ff
pp
ff
p
pp
sempre f
sempre f

33

34

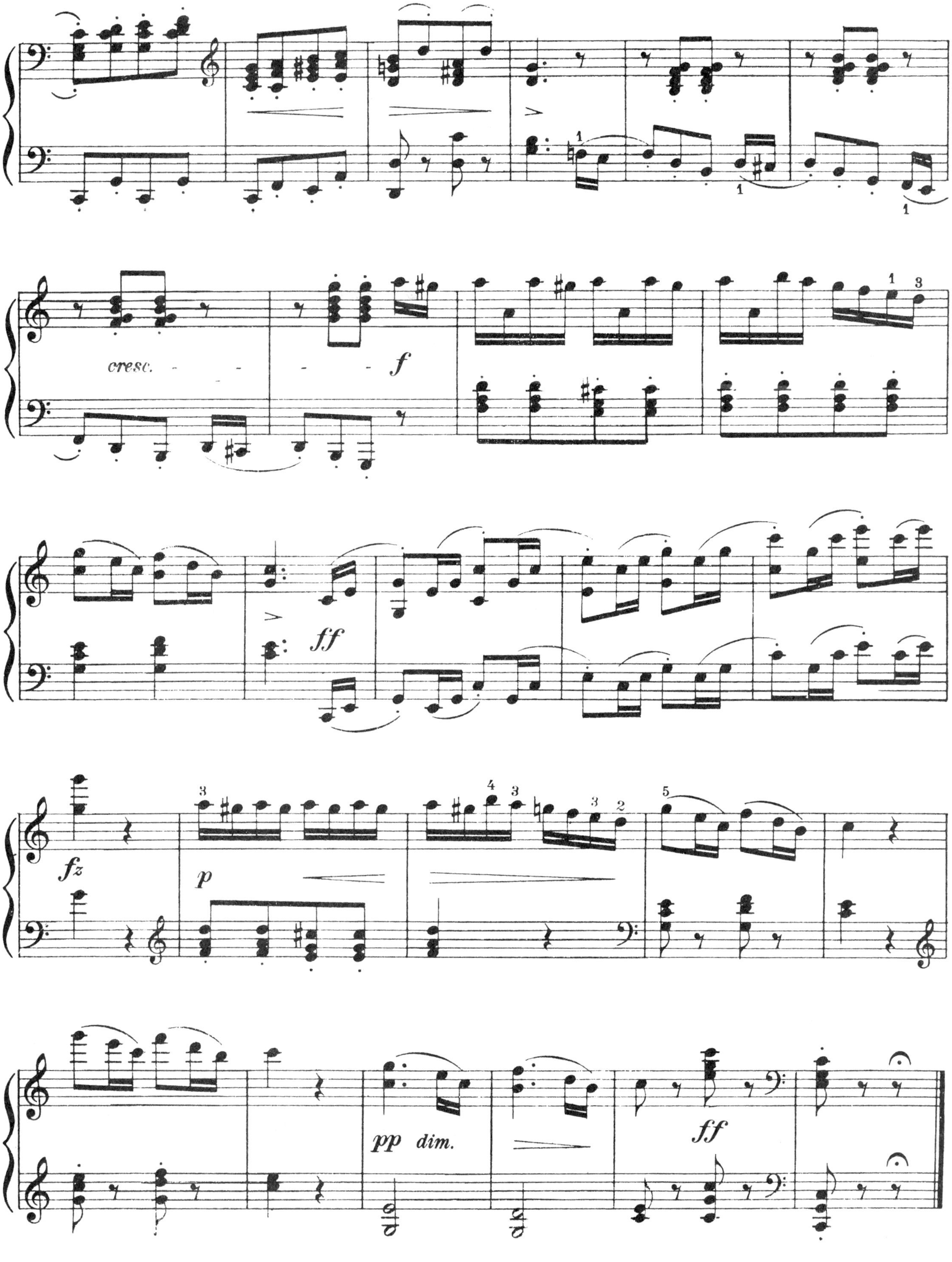
cresc.
f
ff
fz
p
pp dim.
ff

CONTRA DANCE
II

mf
pp
poco rit.
espressivo
a tempo
f
pp
poco ritard.
espressivo
D.C. al Fine
e poi la Coda
Coda
dolce possibile
dim.
cresc.
pp dim.
Ped.

CONTRA DANCE
III

fz
fz
fz
fz
fz
fz
fz
fz
dim.
dolce, più tranquillo
pp
dolce, sempre tranquillo
ritard.
a tempo

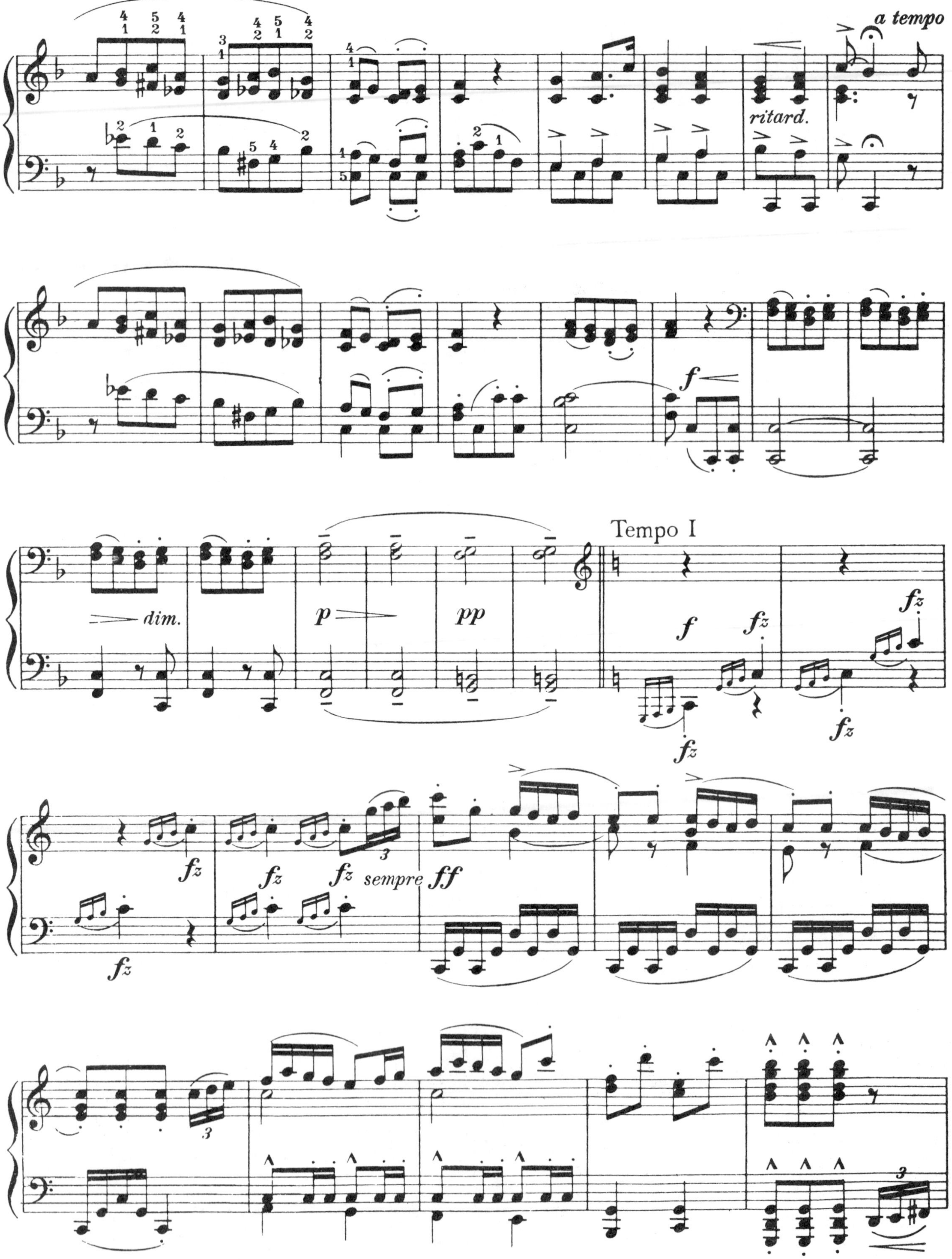
a tempo
ritard.
dim.
Tempo I
sempre ff

41

ECOSSAISE

breve
p
senza ritenuto
f senza affrettando
poco più animato
mf
dim.
p

ancora tranquillo
mf
Ped.
p
mf
poco
fz
Ped.
allarg.
a tempo
f
animato
mf
dim.
a tempo
p
espressivo
p
poco riten.
Ped.

poco a poco accel.
al Tempo I°
p
cresc.
f risoluto
fz
con grazia
p
mf
legg.
poco rit.
a tempo
cresc. molto
f
p subito
dim.
pp

46

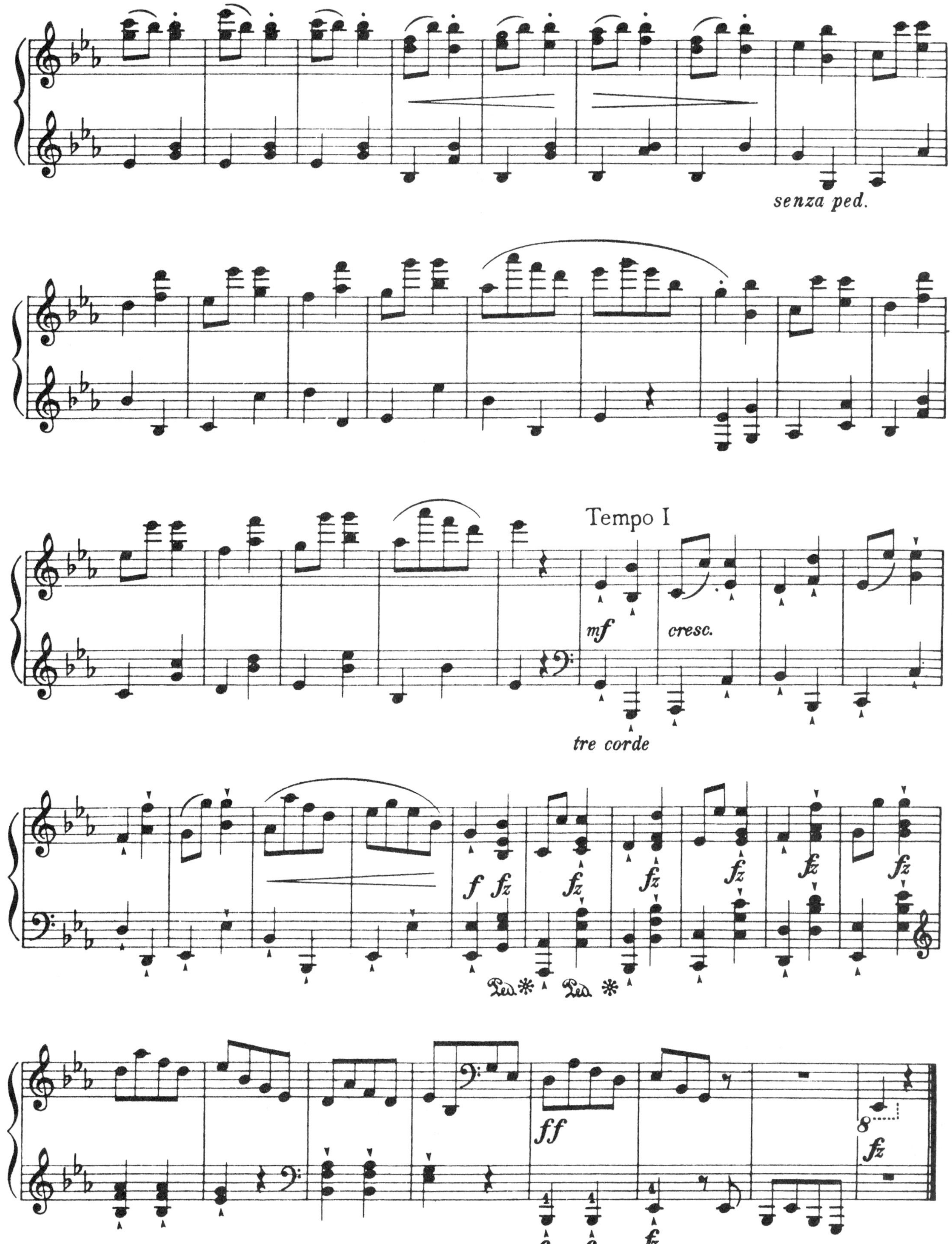
senza ped.
Tempo I
mf
cresc.
tre corde
f
fz
ff

GERMAN DANCE
I

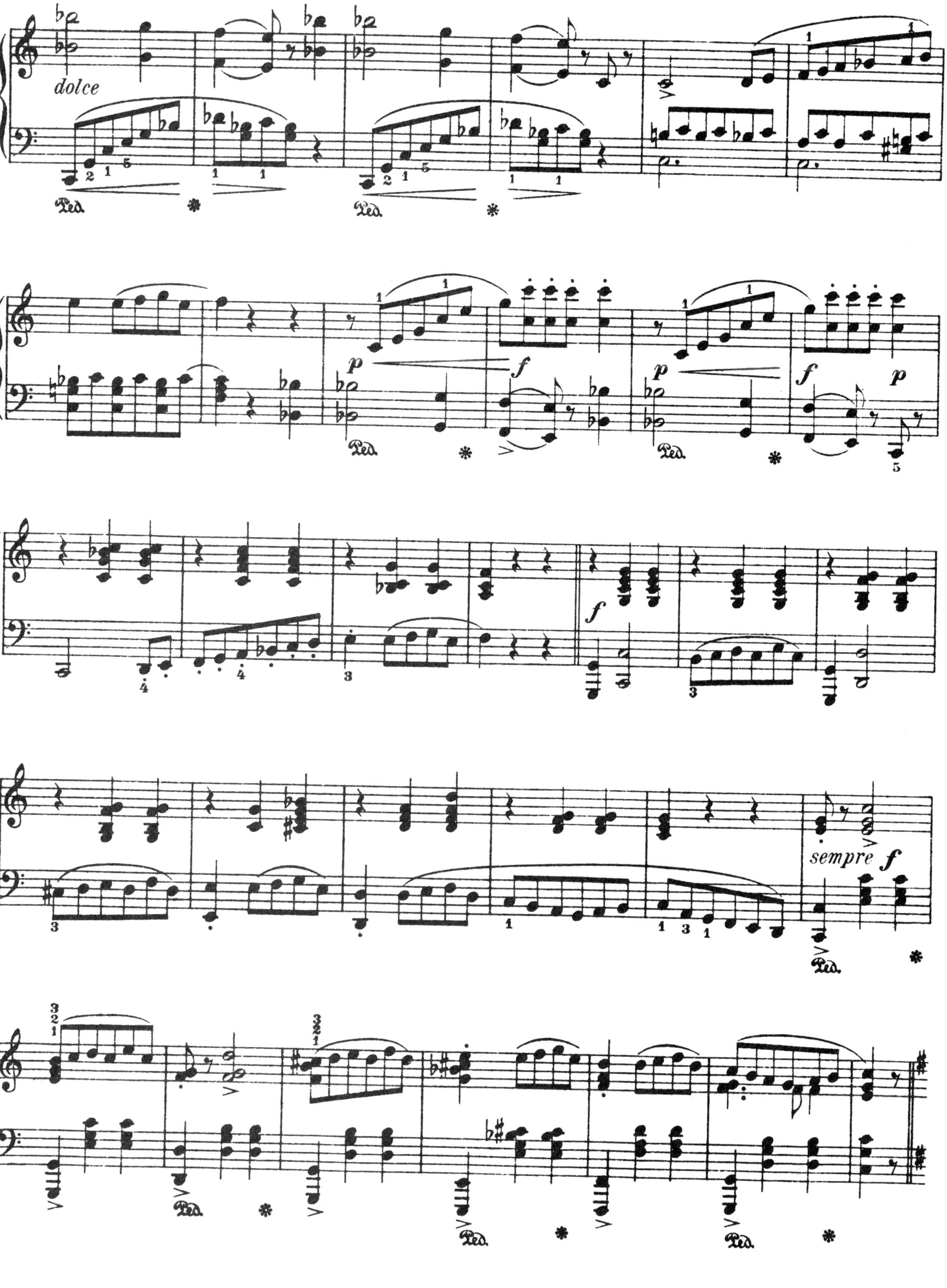
dolce
sempre f

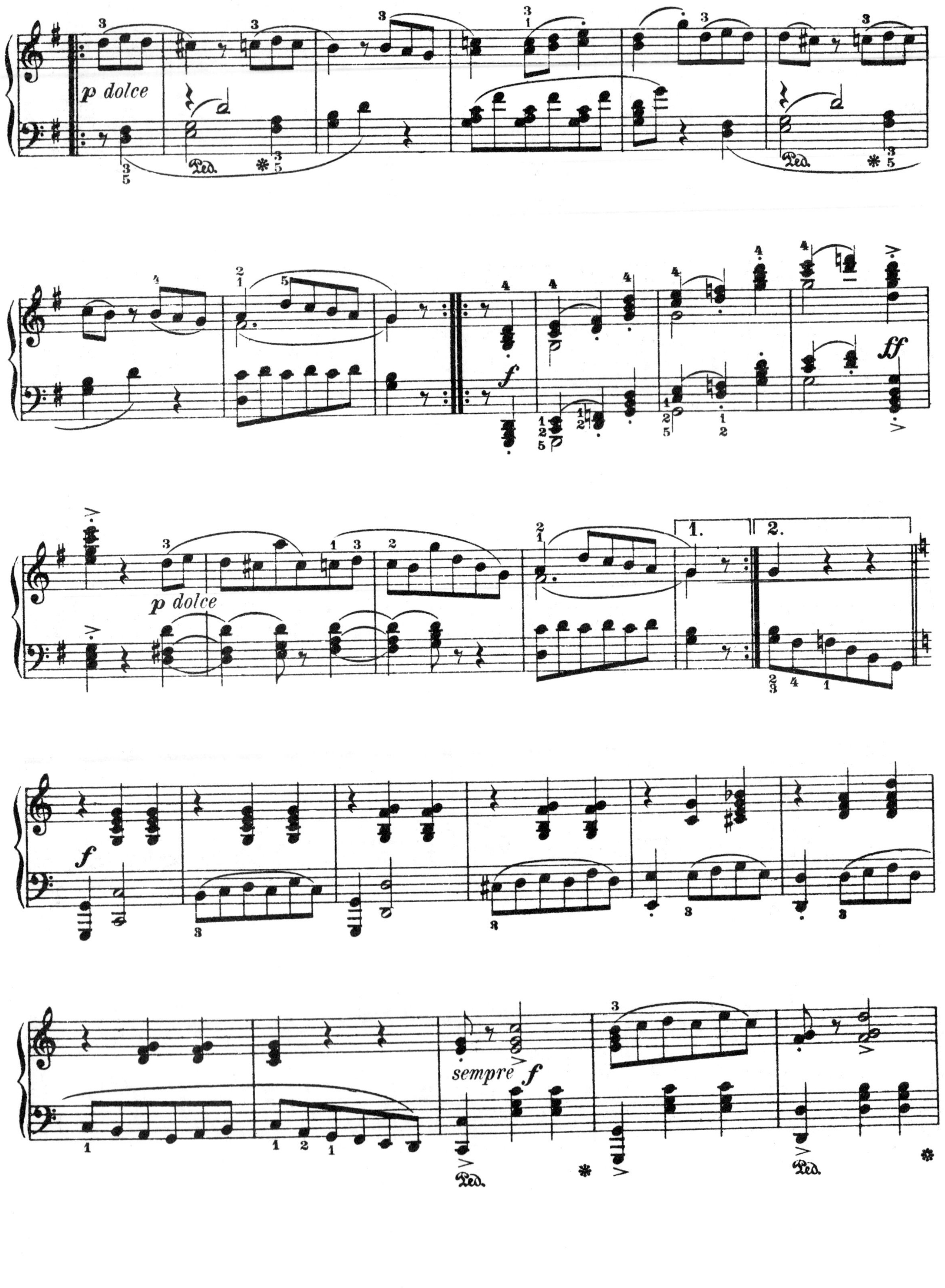
p dolce
Ped.
Ped.
f
ff
p dolce
1.
2.
f
sempre f
Ped.
Ped.

51

Coda

GERMAN DANCE
II

Allegretto grazioso ♩= 138

53

mf espressivo
pp sotto
poco ritard.
a tempo
mf
pp sotto
1.
2.
p dolce

Coda

GERMAN DANCE
III

Più lento e molto grazioso

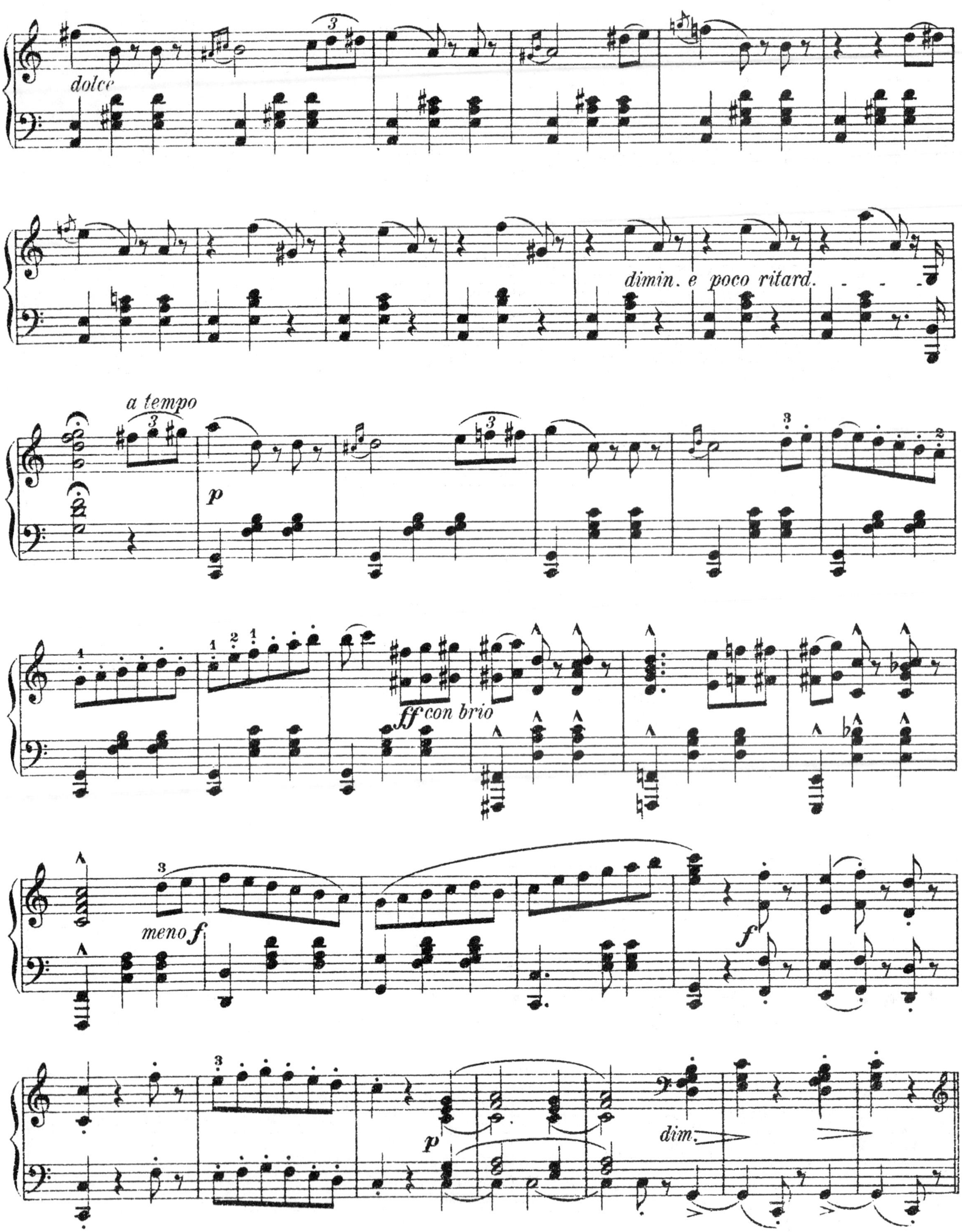
dolce
dimin. e poco ritard.
a tempo
p
ff con brio
meno f
f
p
dim.

Poco più lento
p espressivo
sempre p
cresc.
f
mf
più cresc.
ff
p ad libitum

60

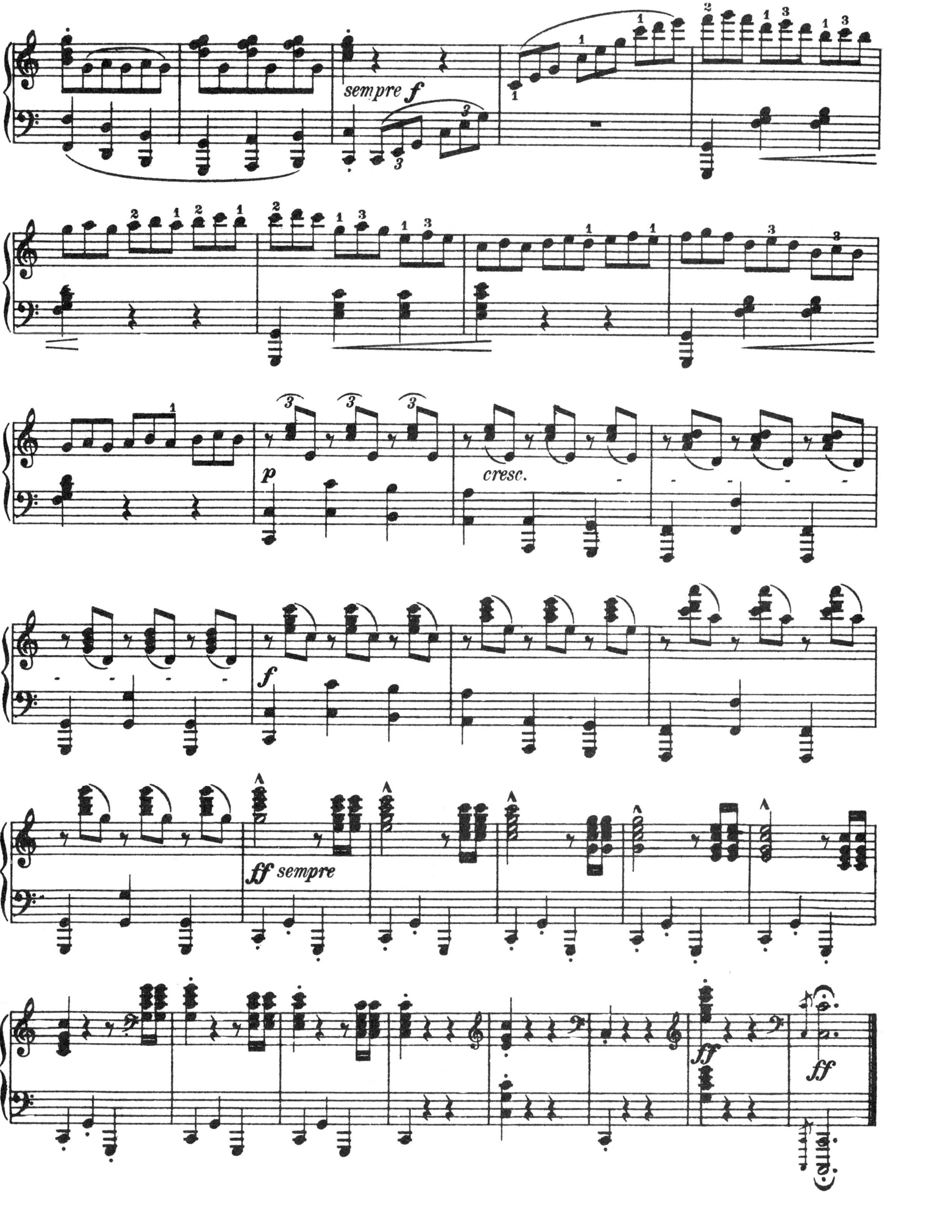
sempre f
p
cresc.
f
ff sempre
ff
ff

SONATA
Opus 2
II

MENUETTO
Allegretto

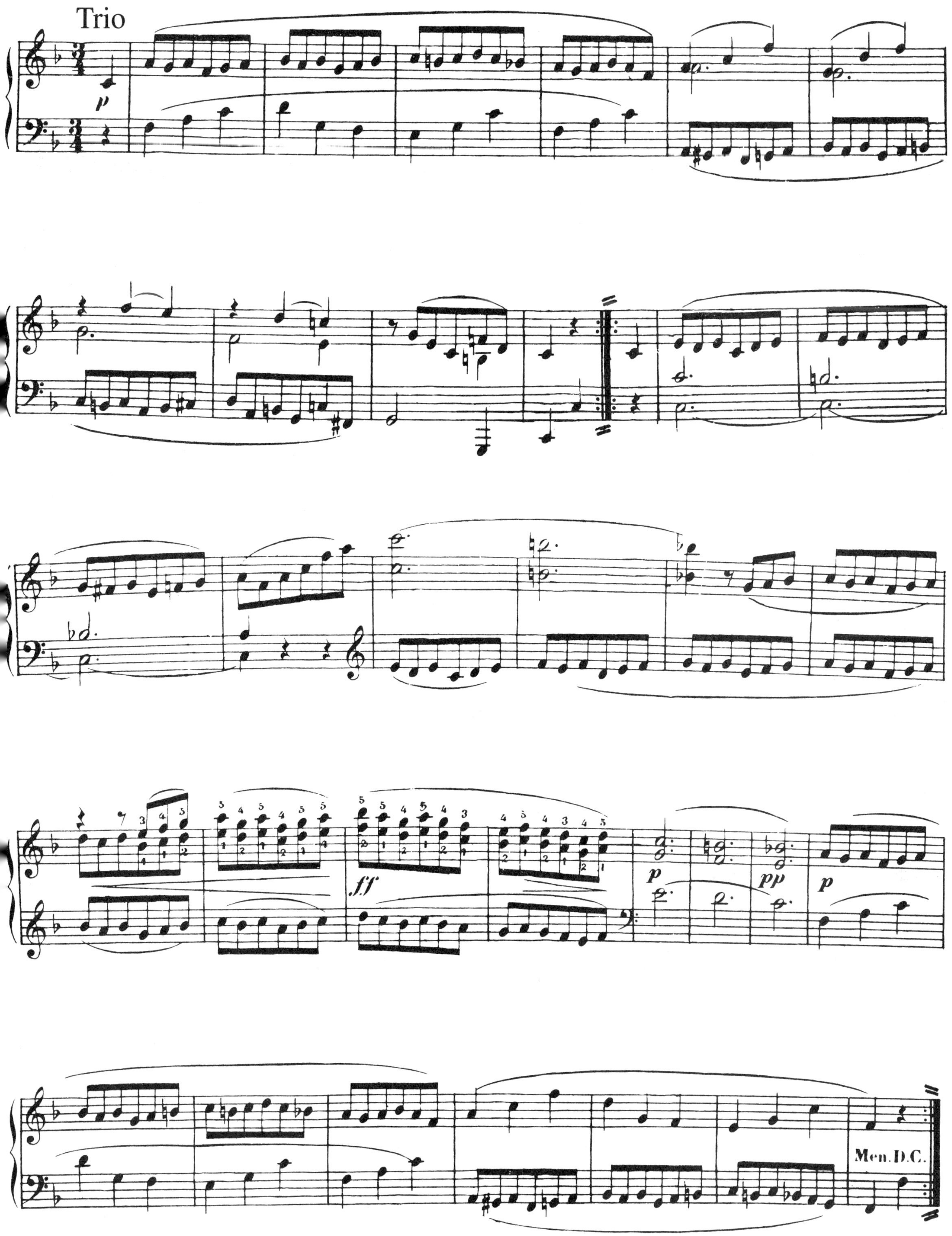
Trio
p
ff
p
pp
p
Men. D.C.

SONATA
Opus 7
III

Allegro

65

SONATA
Opus 10, No. 2
II

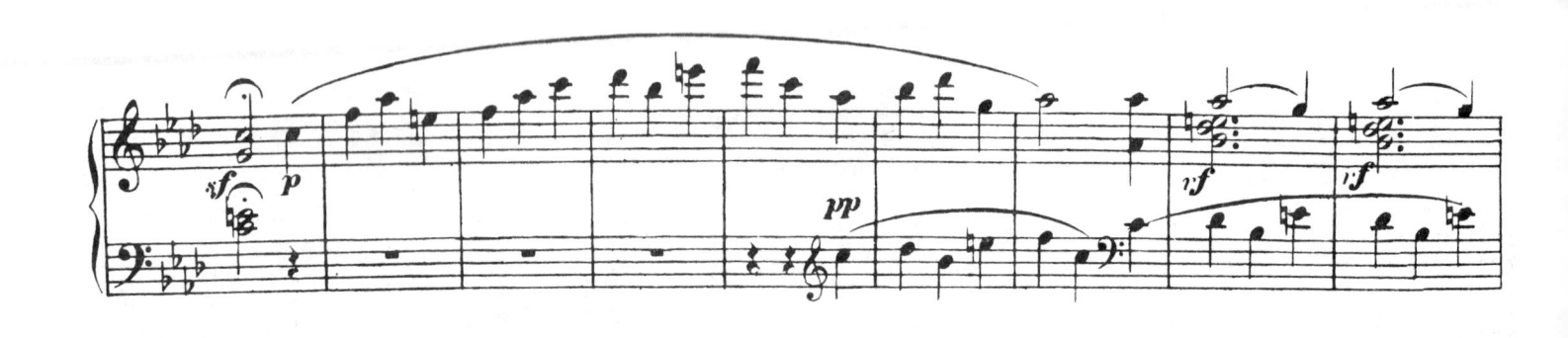

Allegretto

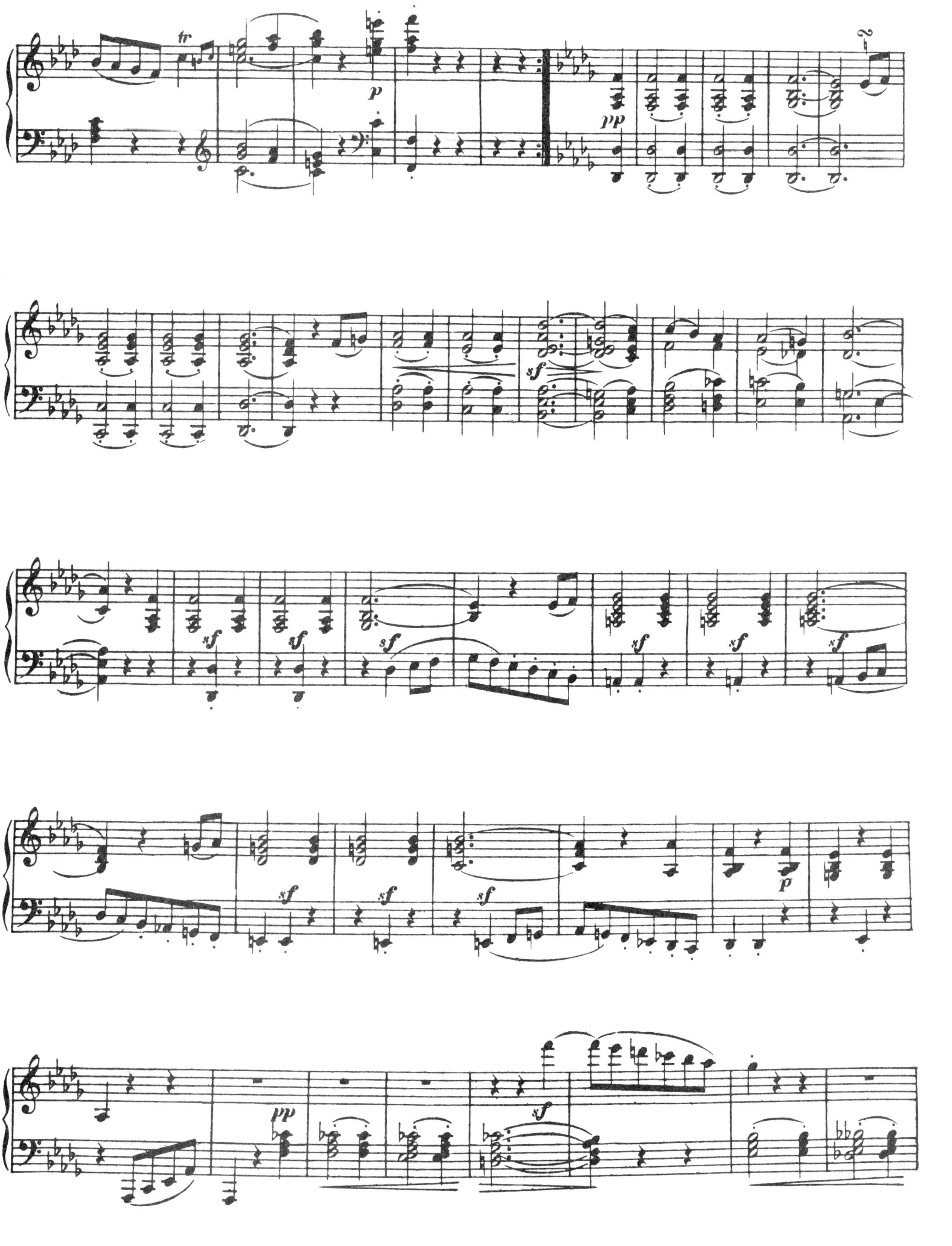
tr
p
pp
sf
p
pp
sf

sf
sf
sf
sf
cresc.
sf
sf
sf
sf
pp
pp
pp
sf
sf
sf
sf
sf
cresc.
sf
sf
sf
pp
pp
pp
p

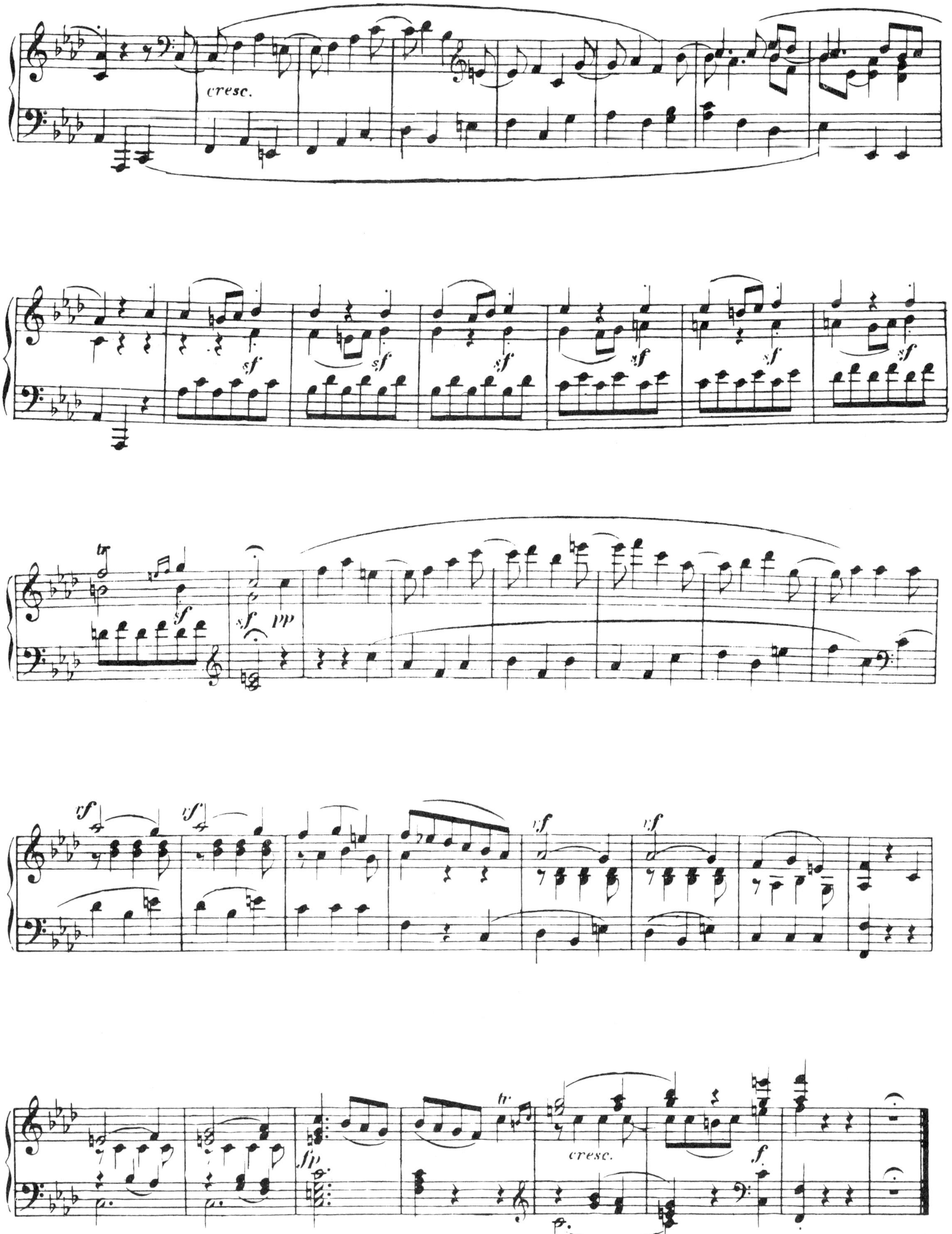
cresc.
sf
tr
pp
rf
fp
cresc.
f

SONATA
Opus 10, No. 3

III

MENUETTO
Allegro

Trio.

Men. D.C. ma senza replica

SONATA
Opus 13
"Pathetique"

attacca subito il Allegro.

Allegro di molto e con brio

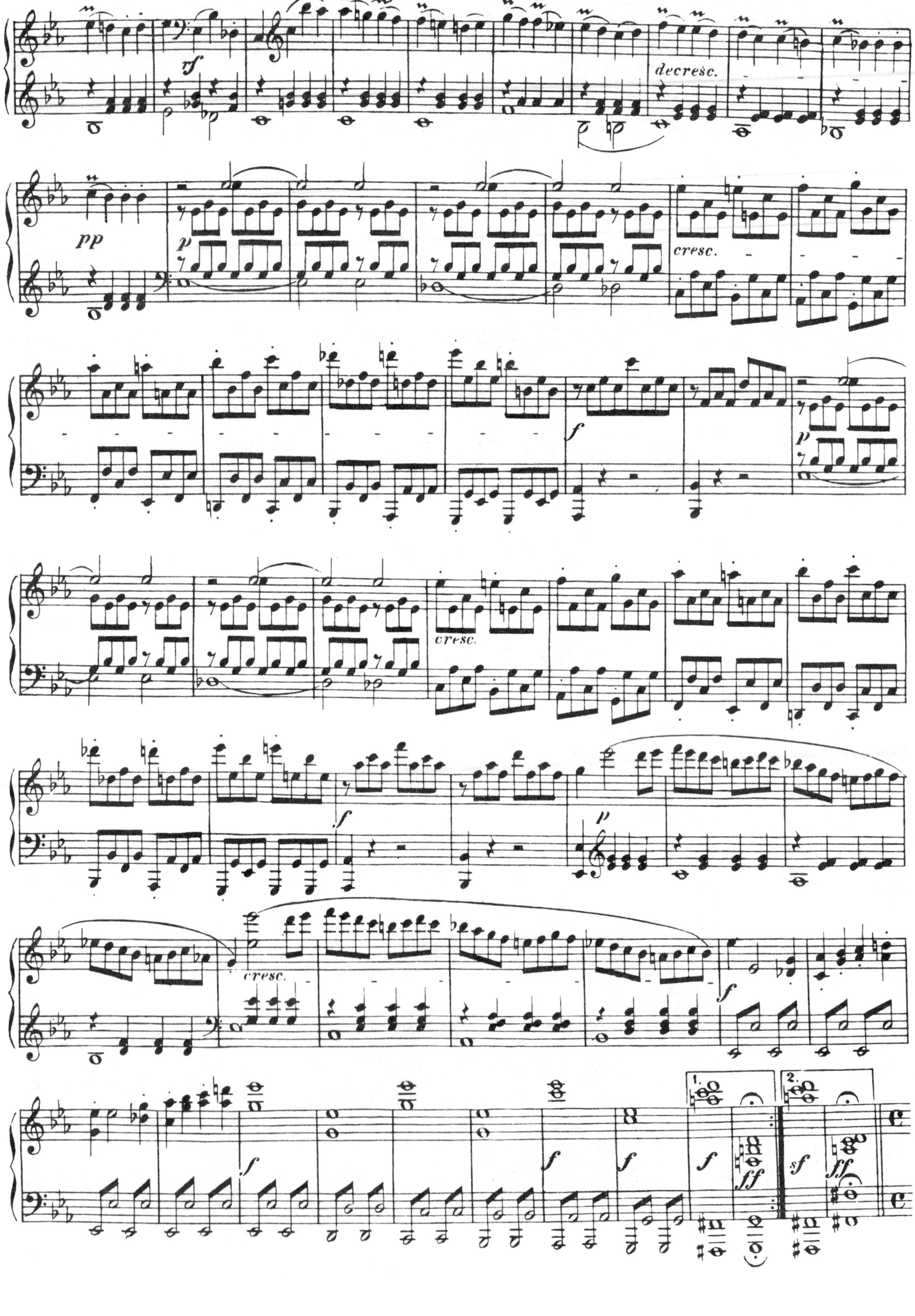
rf
decresc.
pp
p
cresc.
f
p
cresc.
f
p
cresc.
f
f
f
f
f
ff
1.
2.
sf
ff

Tempo I.
fp
fp
fp
p
decresc.
pp
attacca subito Allegro molto e con brio
Allegro molto e con brio
p
cresc.
f
p
cresc.
f
p
cresc.
p
pp
cresc.

sf
pp
cresc.
sf
tr
sf
tr
sf
tr
fp
p
sf
cresc.
p
sf
cresc.
p
cresc.
p
cresc.
p

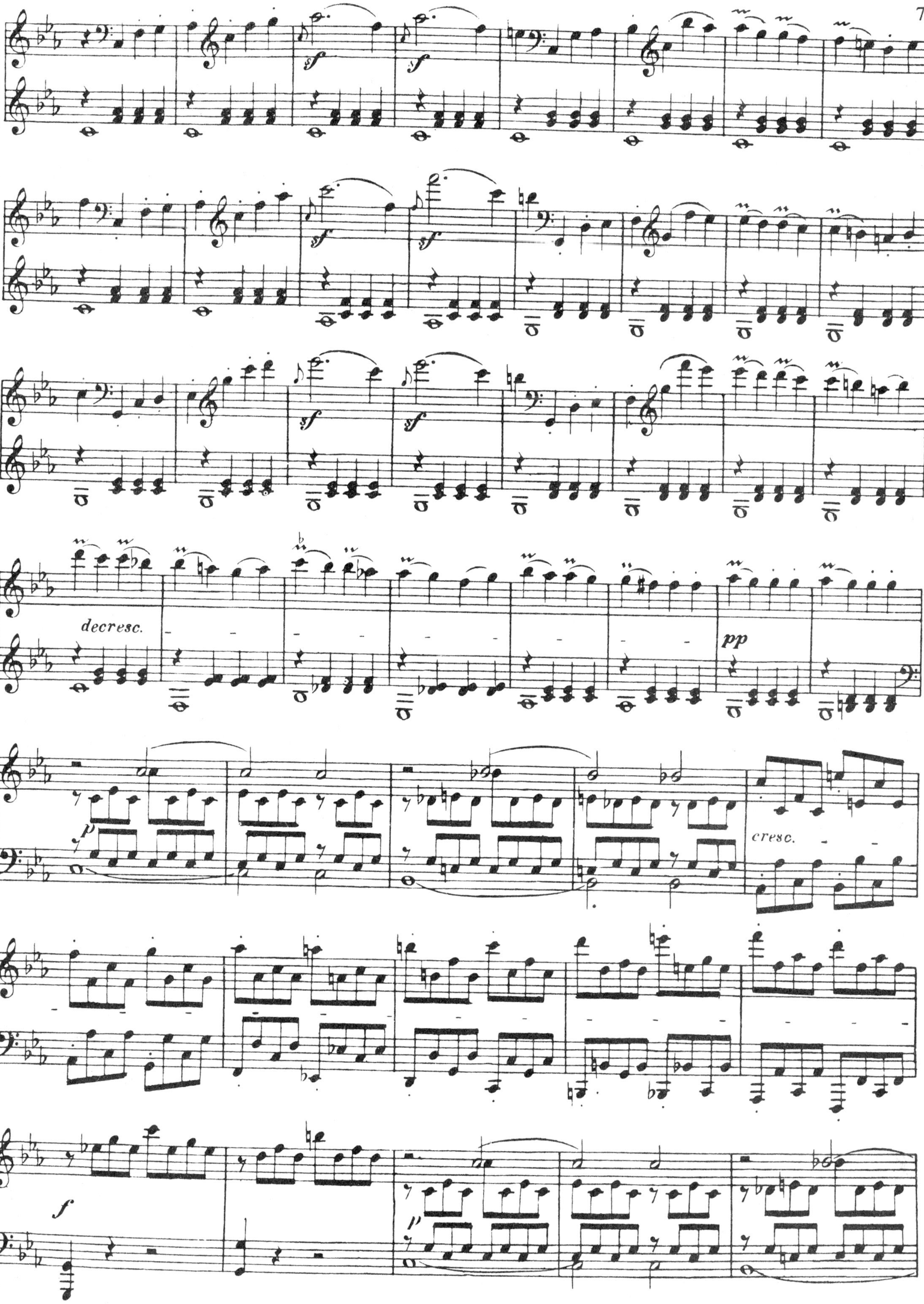
sf
sf
sf
sf
sf
sf
decresc.
pp
p
cresc.
f
p

cresc.
f
[p]
cresc.
f
sf
f
ff
fff
Grave.
p
cresc.
sf
decresc.
pp
Allegro molto e con brio
p
cresc.
ff
ff

Adagio cantabile

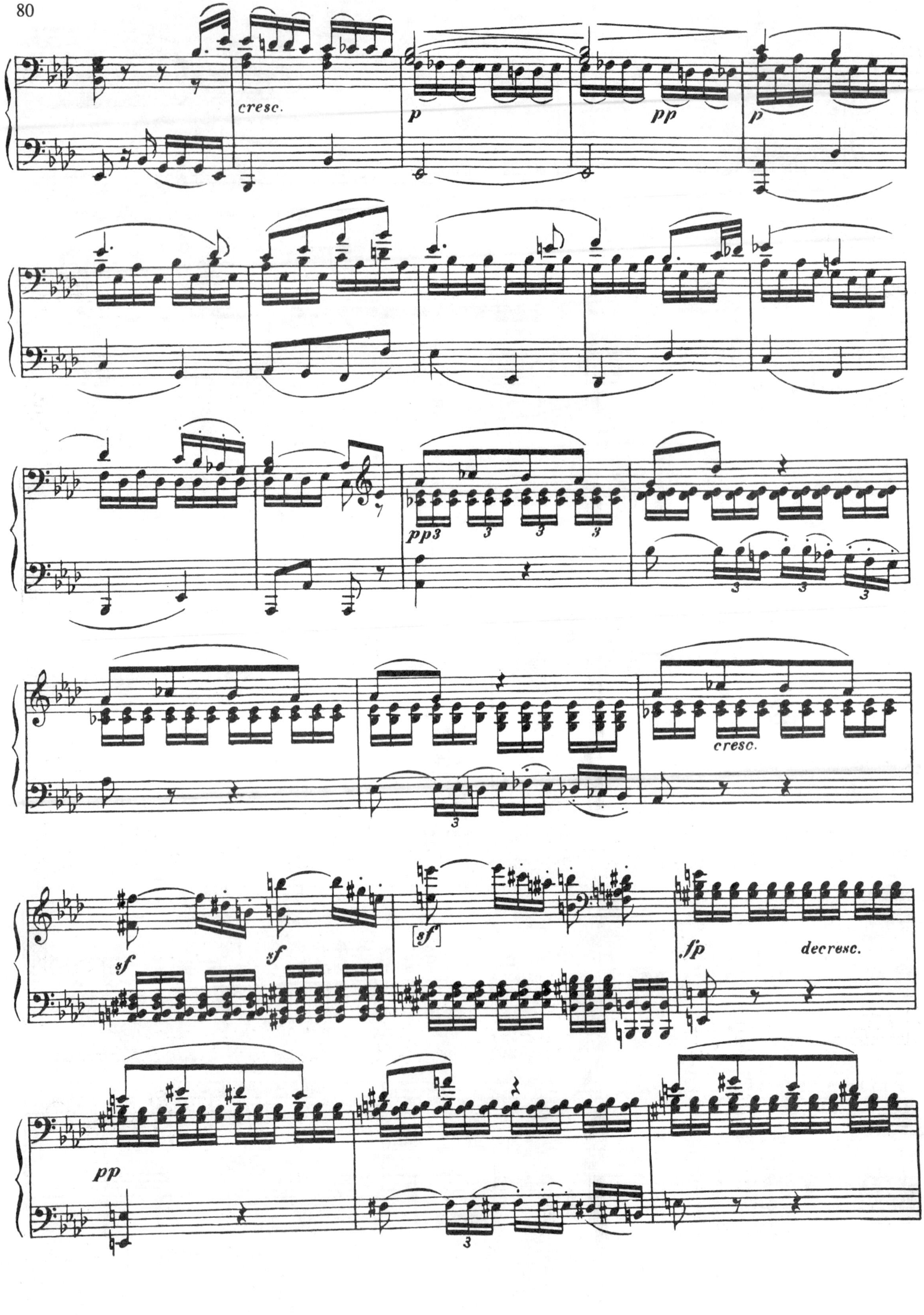
cresc.
p
pp
p
pp
cresc.
sf
sf
[sf]
fp
decresc.
pp

81

RONDO
Allegro

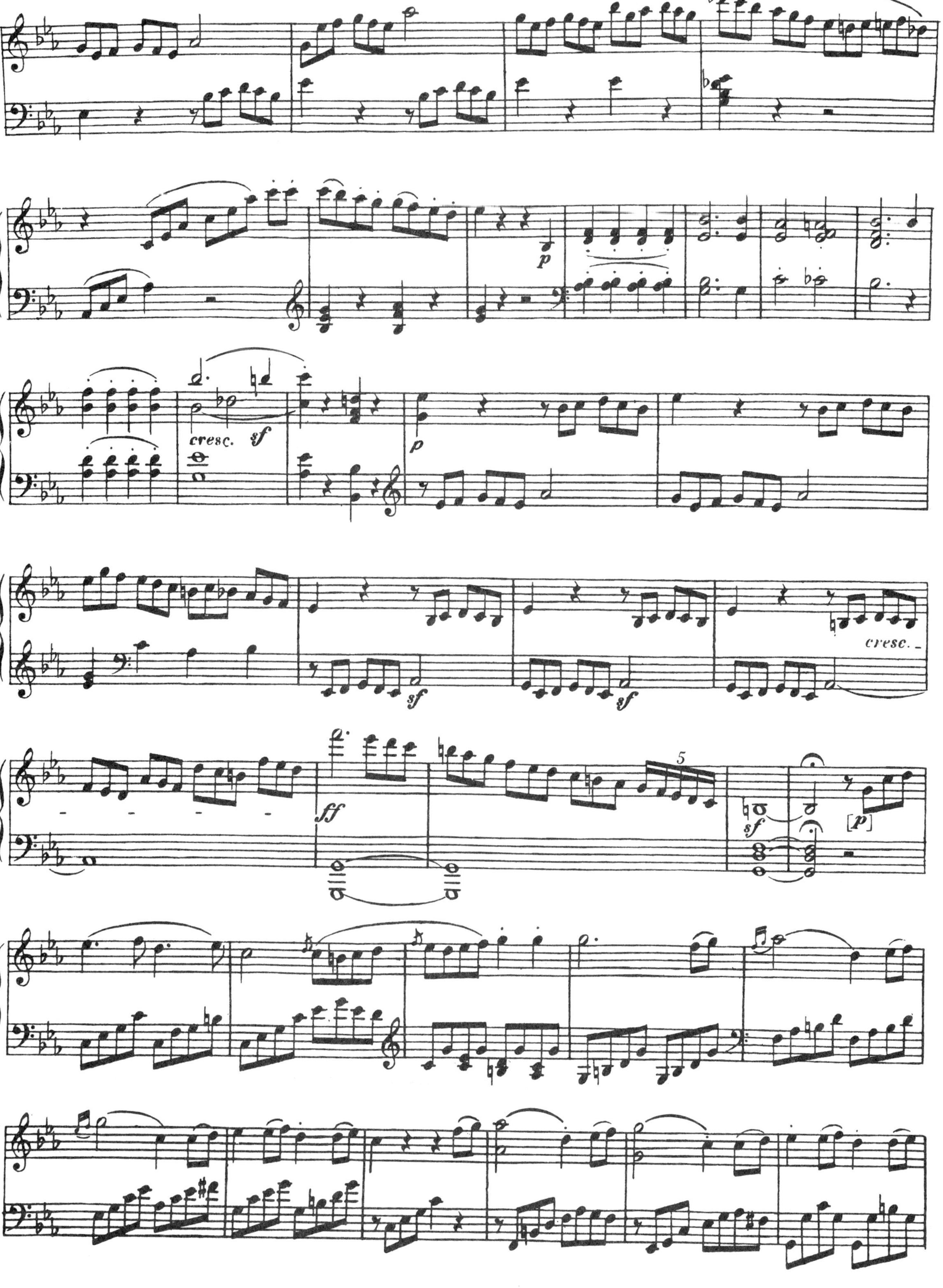
p
cresc.
sf
p
sf
sf
cresc.
ff
5
sf
[p]

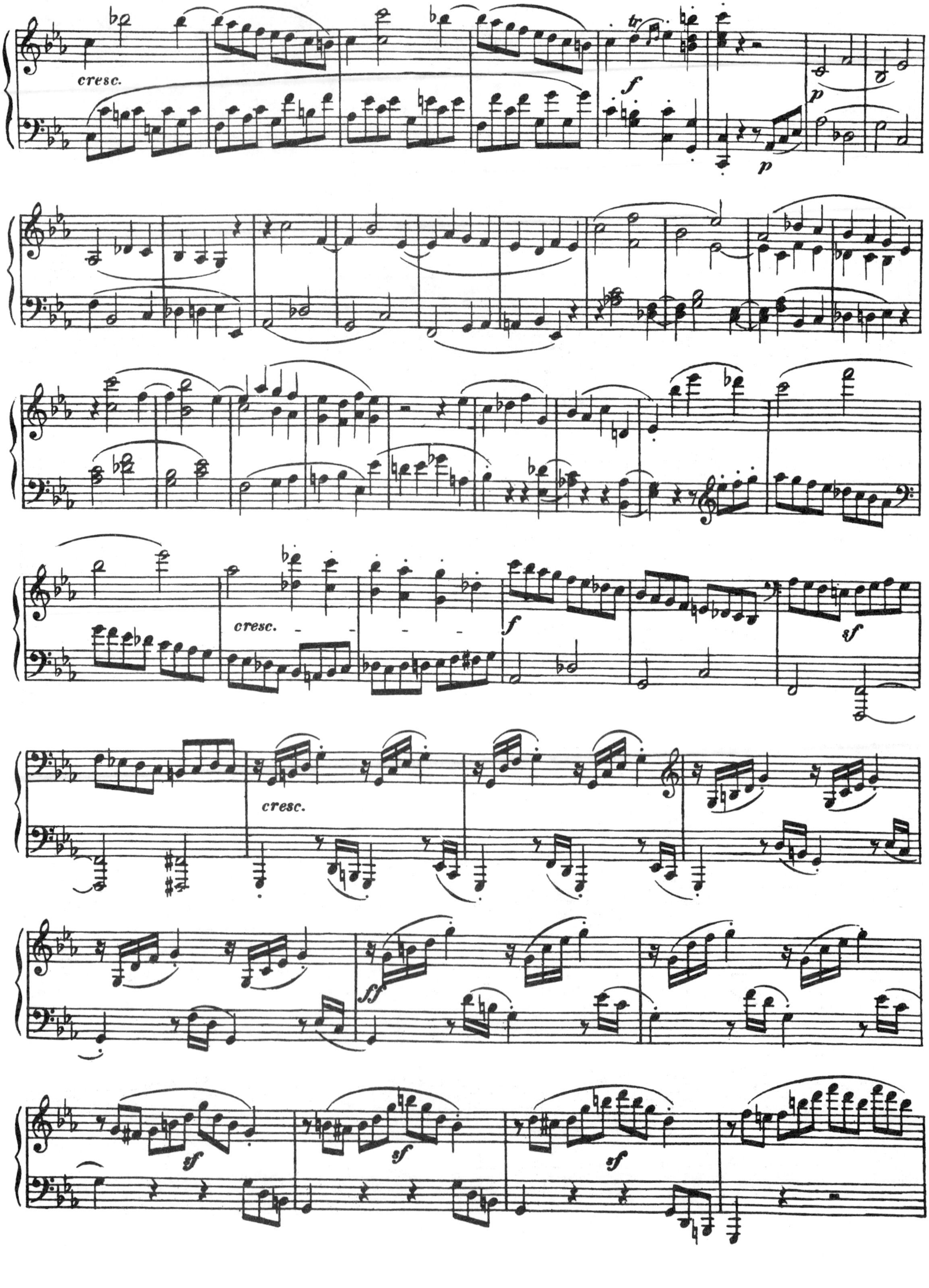
cresc.
tr
f
p
p
cresc.
f
sf
cresc.
ff
sf
sf
sf

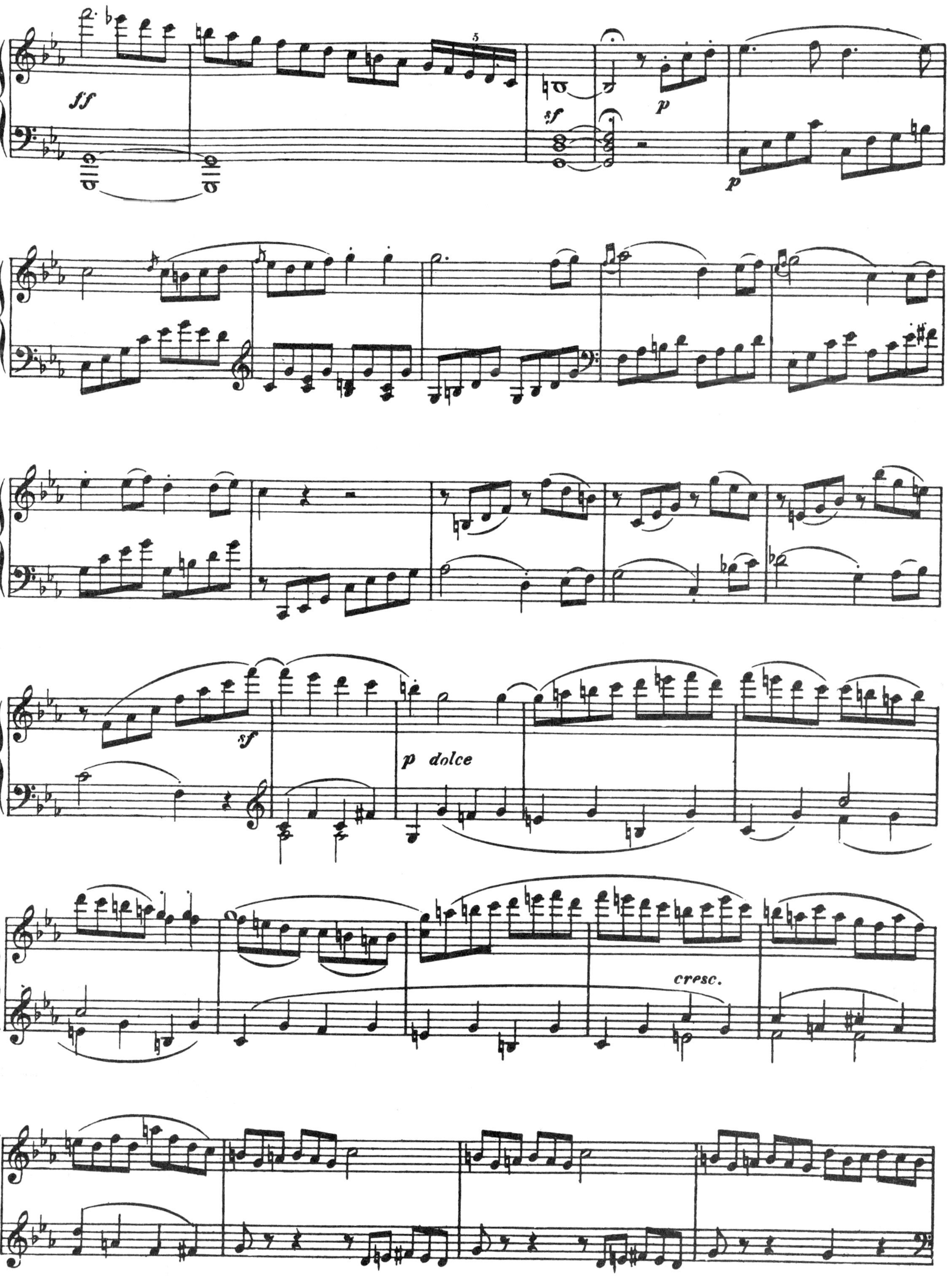

ff
sf
p
p
sf
p dolce
cresc.

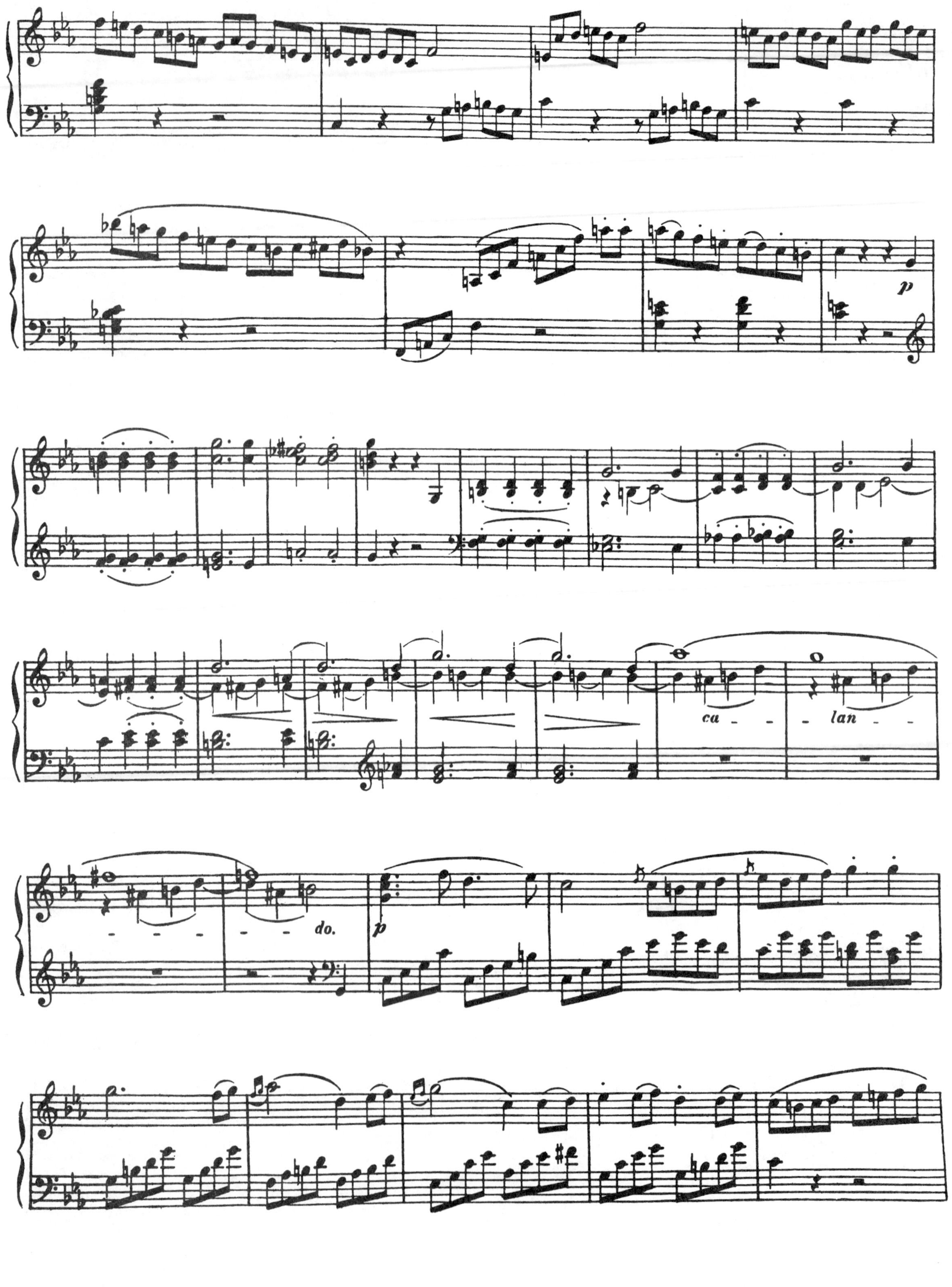
p
ca
lan
do.
p

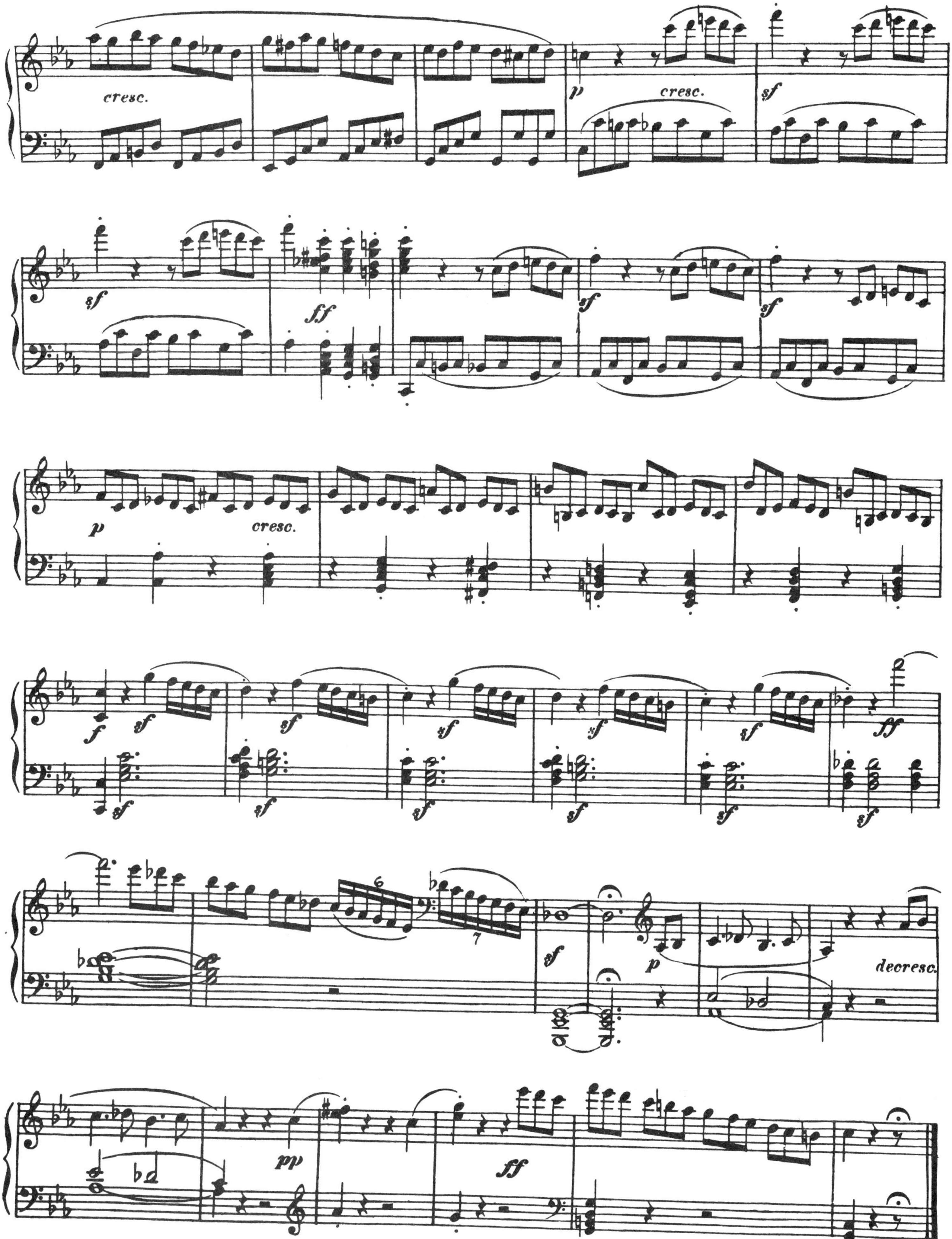
cresc.
p
cresc.
sf
sf
ff
sf
sf
p
cresc.
f
sf
ff
6
7
sf
p
decresc.
pp
ff

SONATA
Opus 27, No. 2
"Moonlight"

Adagio Sostenuto

sempre pp e senza sordino

89

90

sempre legatissimo

attacca subito il seguente

Allegretto

pp
fp
fp
cresc.
pp
dolce
p
p
mf
p
mf
p
espress.
cresc.
sf
p
p
pp
dolce
p
cresc.
rit.
sf
a tempo
pp
attacca subito
il seguente

III Presto Agitato

(𝅗𝅥 = 88)

p
3
cresc.
poco
a
poco
sf
f
tr
sf
sf
sf
tr
sf
ff
p
cresc.
p
tr
ff
p
cresc.
f

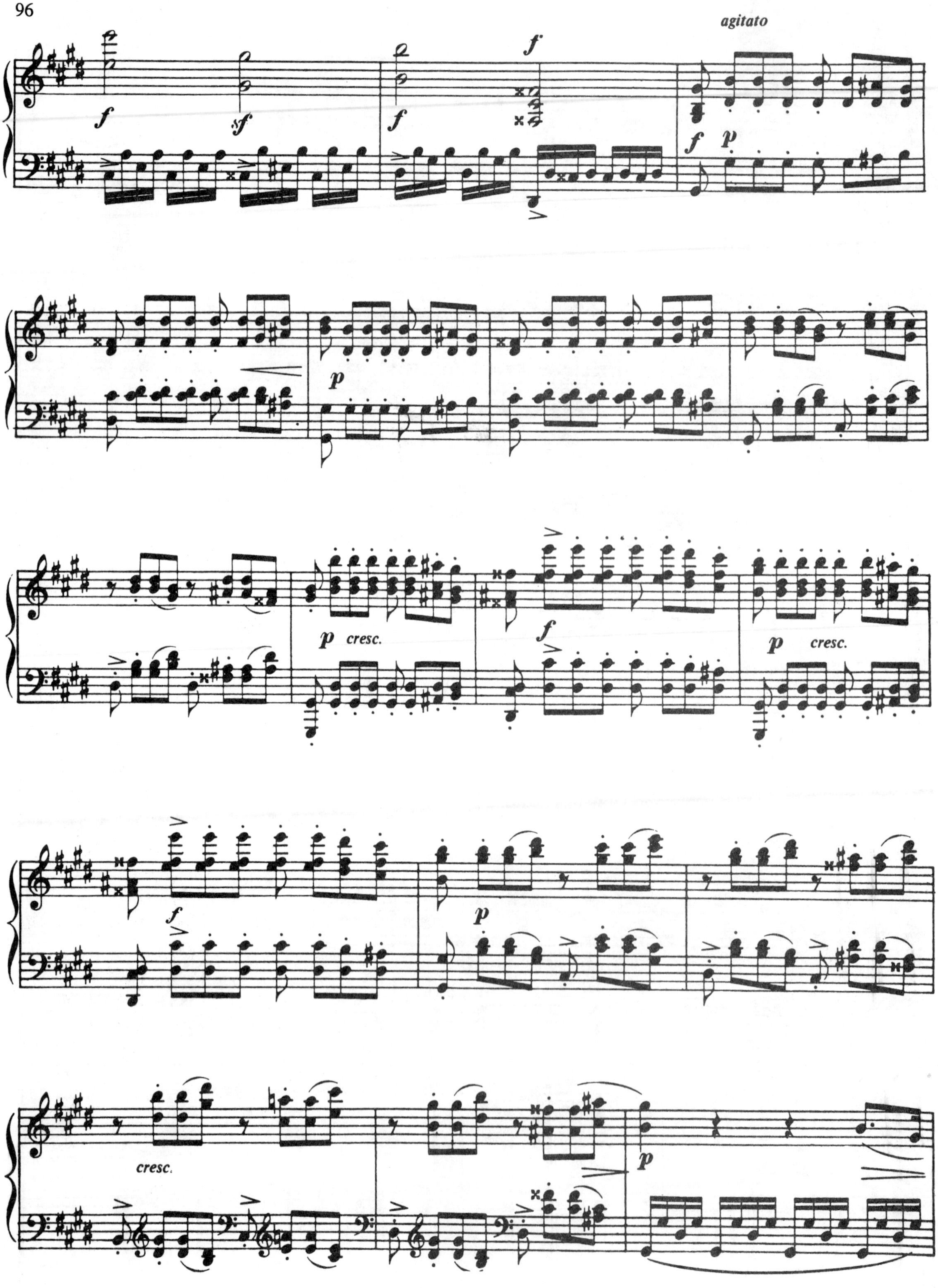
agitato
f
sf
f
f
f
p
p
cresc.
p
cresc.
f
p
cresc.
f
p
cresc.
p

97

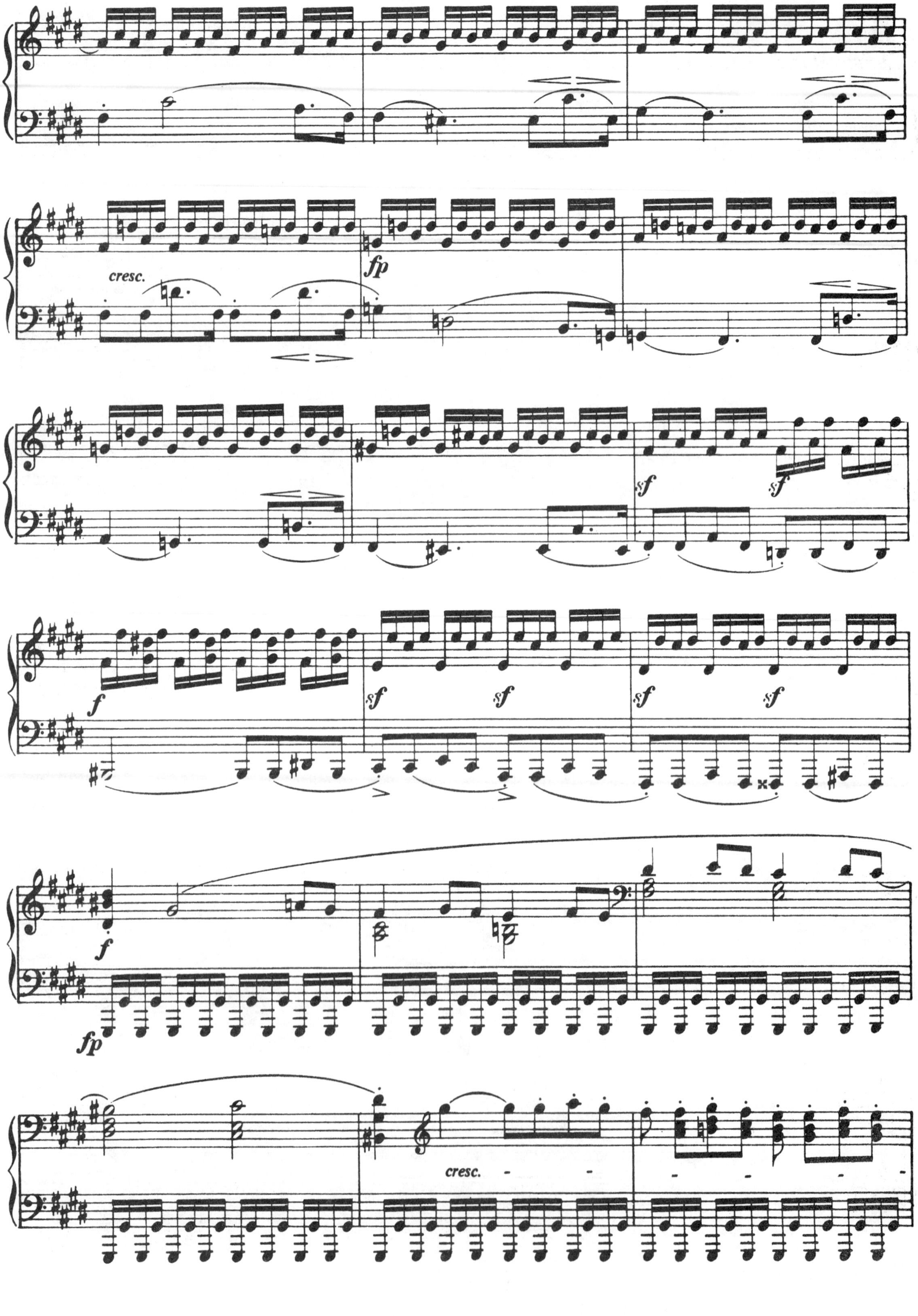
cresc.
fp
sf
sf
f
sf
sf
sf
sf
f
fp
cresc.

tranquillo
p
rit.
molto tranquillo
ten.
ten.
p
pp
una
corda
sf
p
sf p
sf p
sfz p
sfz p
sfz f
f
dim.
sf
cresc.
ten.
sf
lunga
f
sf

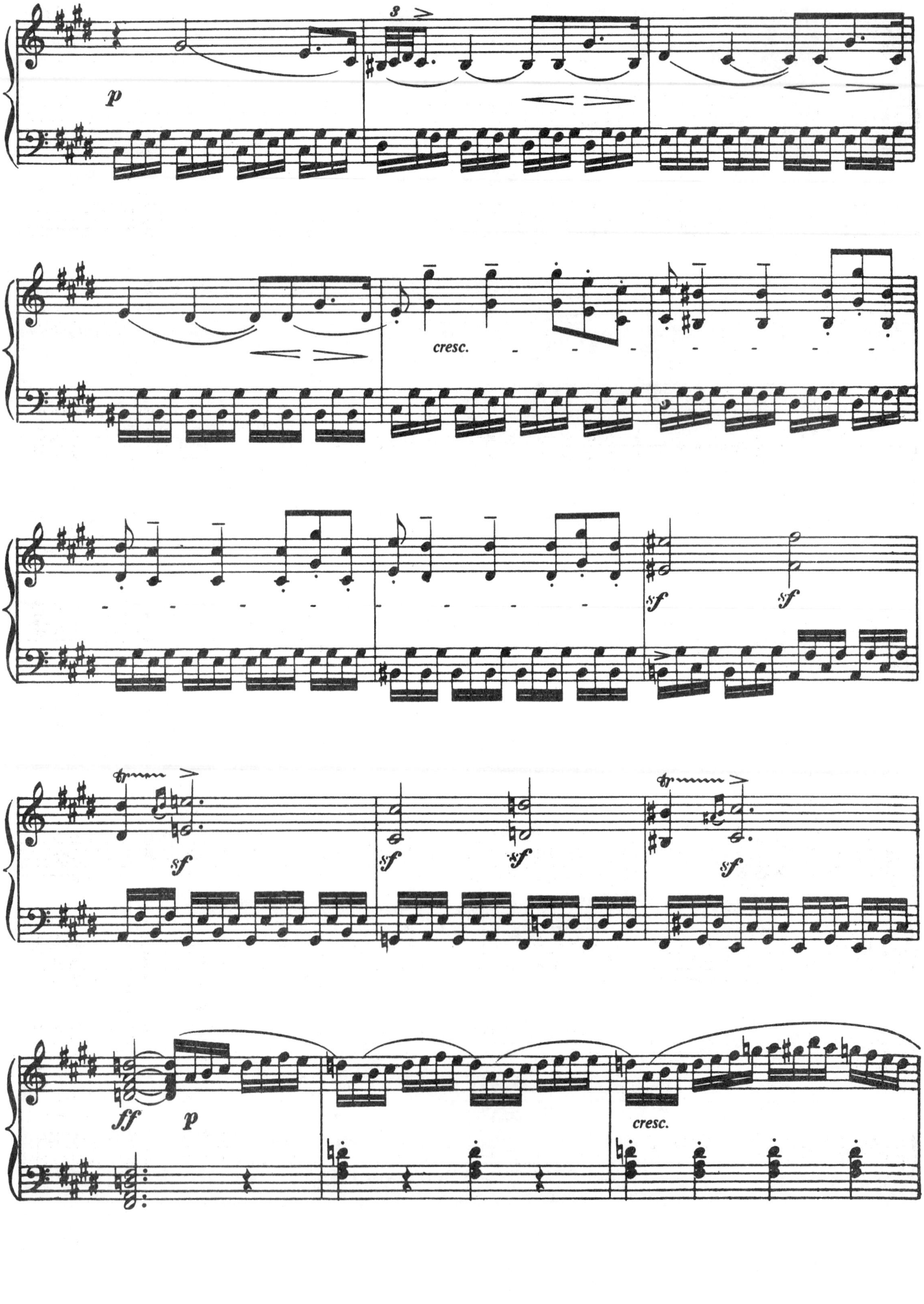
p
cresc.
sf
sf
sf
sf
sf
sf
ff
p
cresc.

tr
p
ff
p
cresc.
ten.
ff
sfz
sfz
sfz
f
p
p
cresc.
f
sf
sf
sf
f
p
piu tranquillo espress.
cresc.
decresc.
p

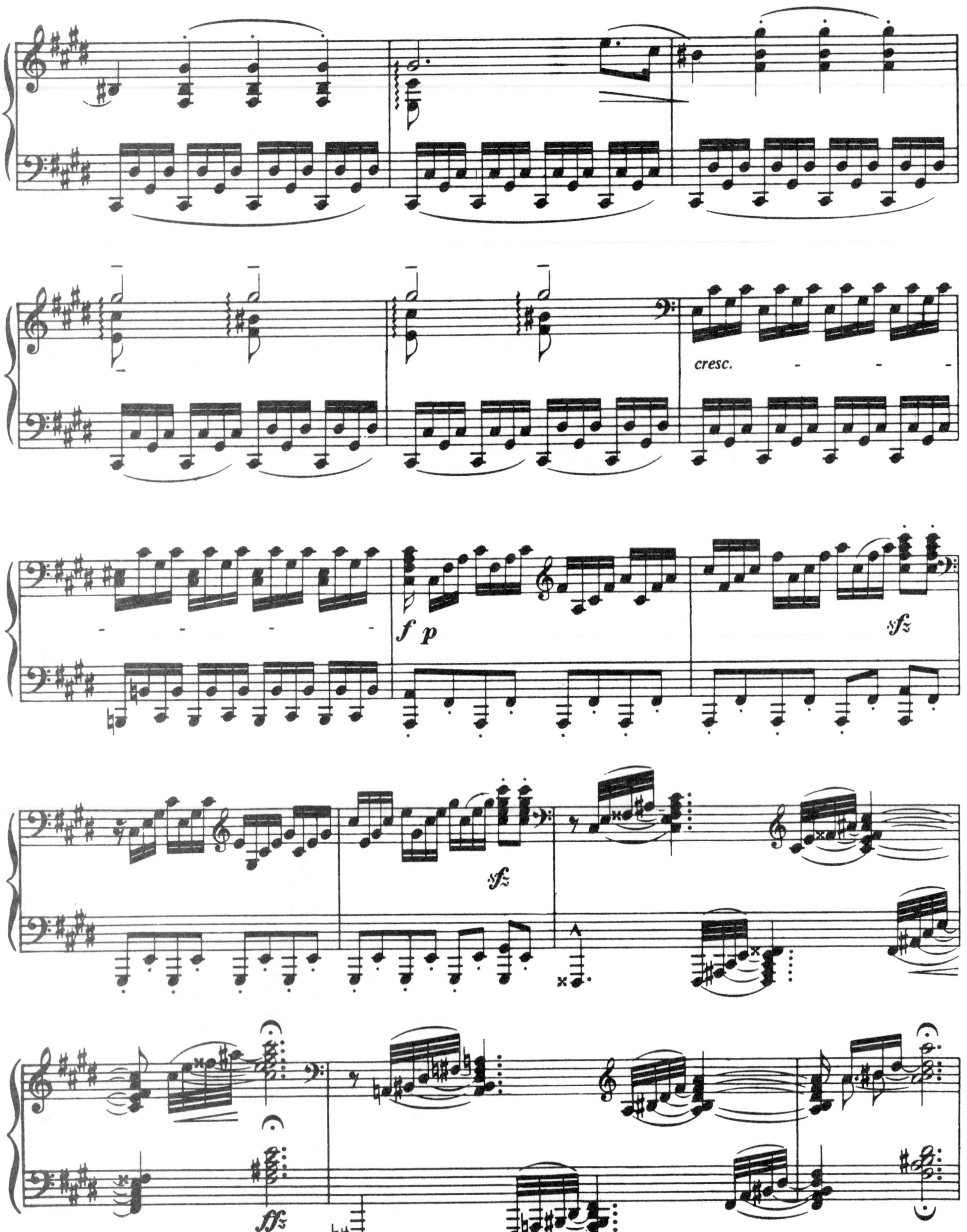
cresc.
f
p
sfz
sfz
sfz
ffz

pp
p
espress., ma non troppo appassionato
ten.
p
ten.
cresc.
f
più f

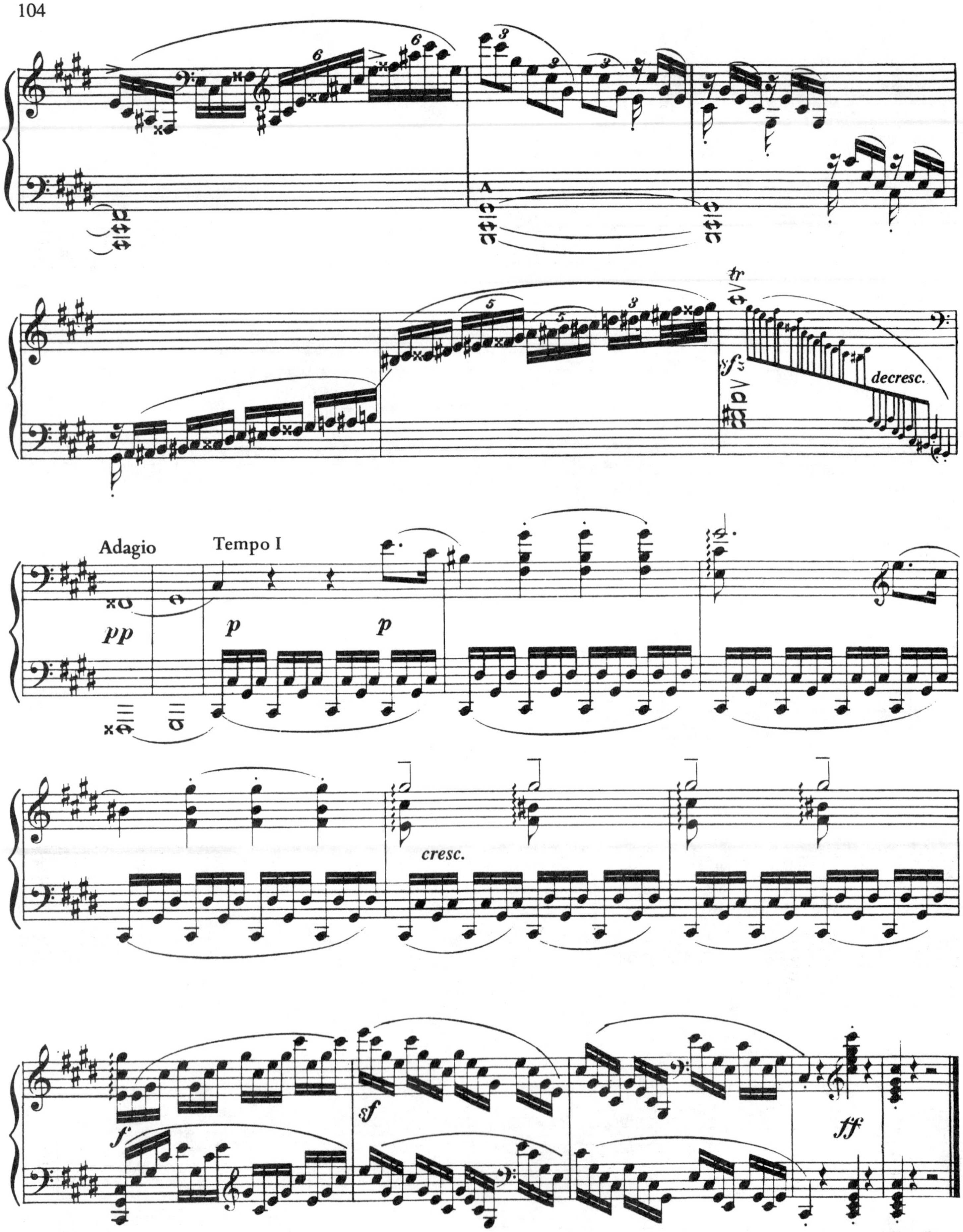
tr
decresc.
Adagio
Tempo I
pp
p
p
cresc.
f
sf
ff

SONATA
Opus 28
III

SCHERZO
Allegro vivace

La seconda parte una volta

Scherzo da capo.

SONATA
Opus 49, No. 1

Andante

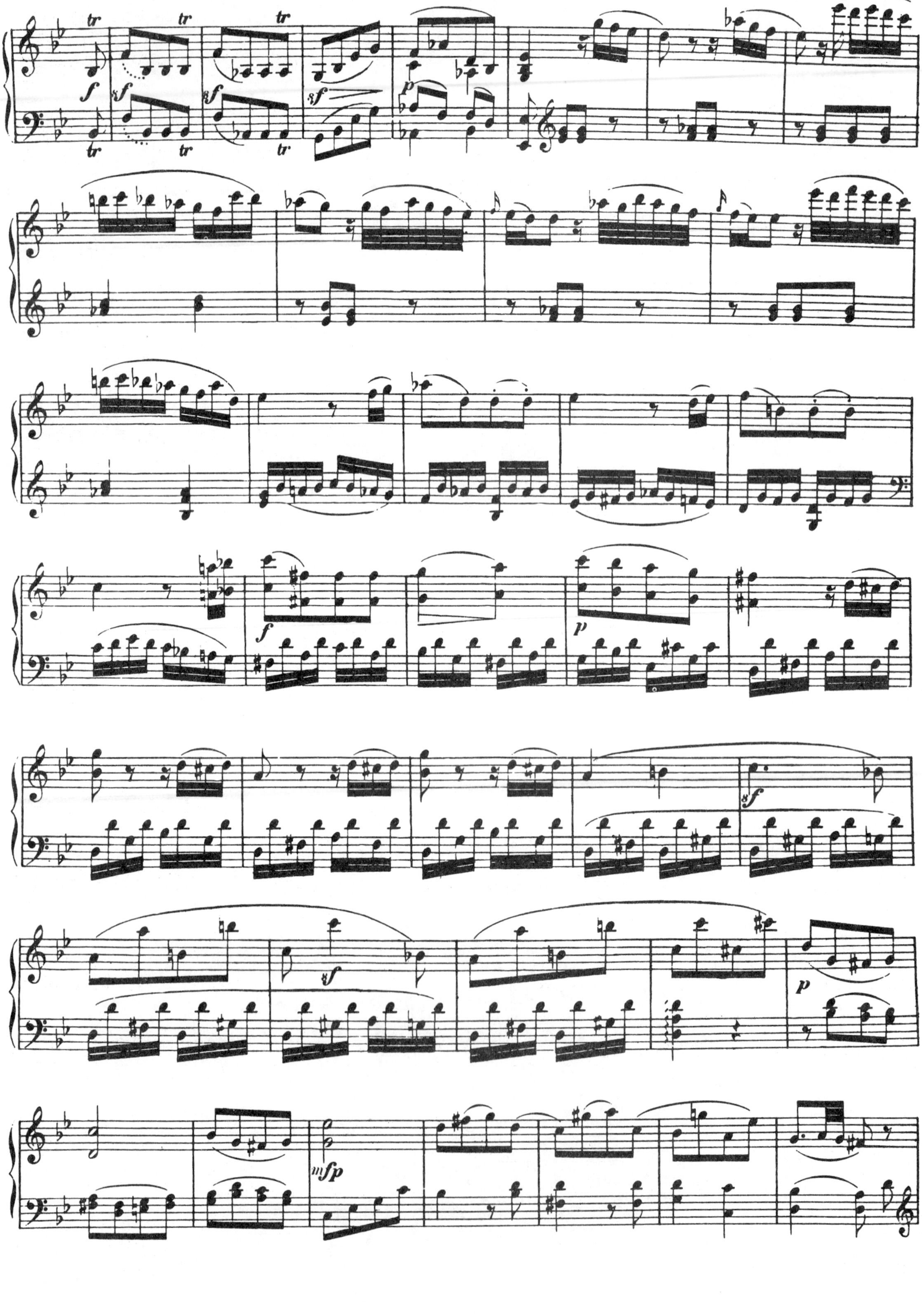
tr
f
sf
p
mfp

109

Rondo
Allegro

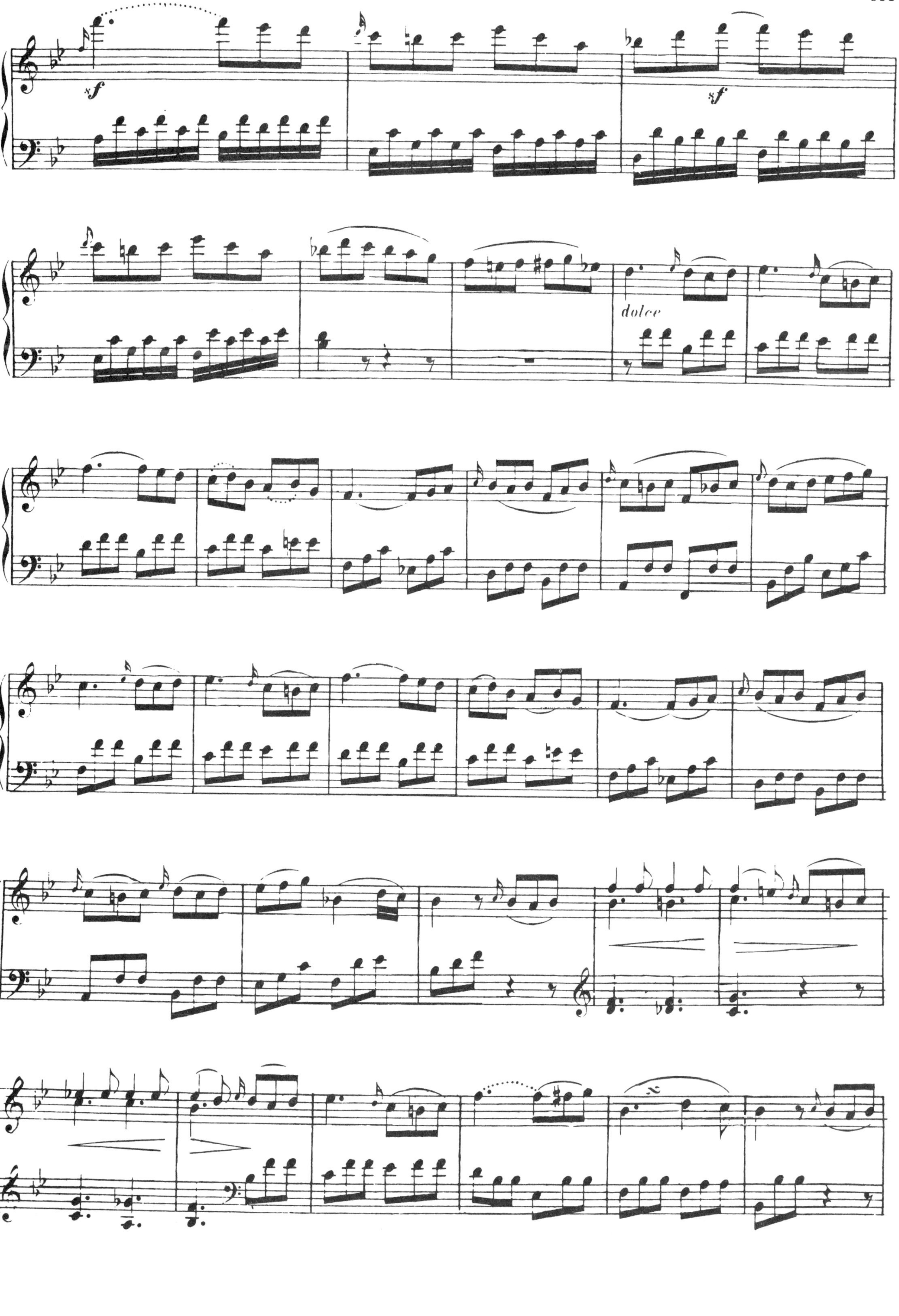
sf
sf
dolce

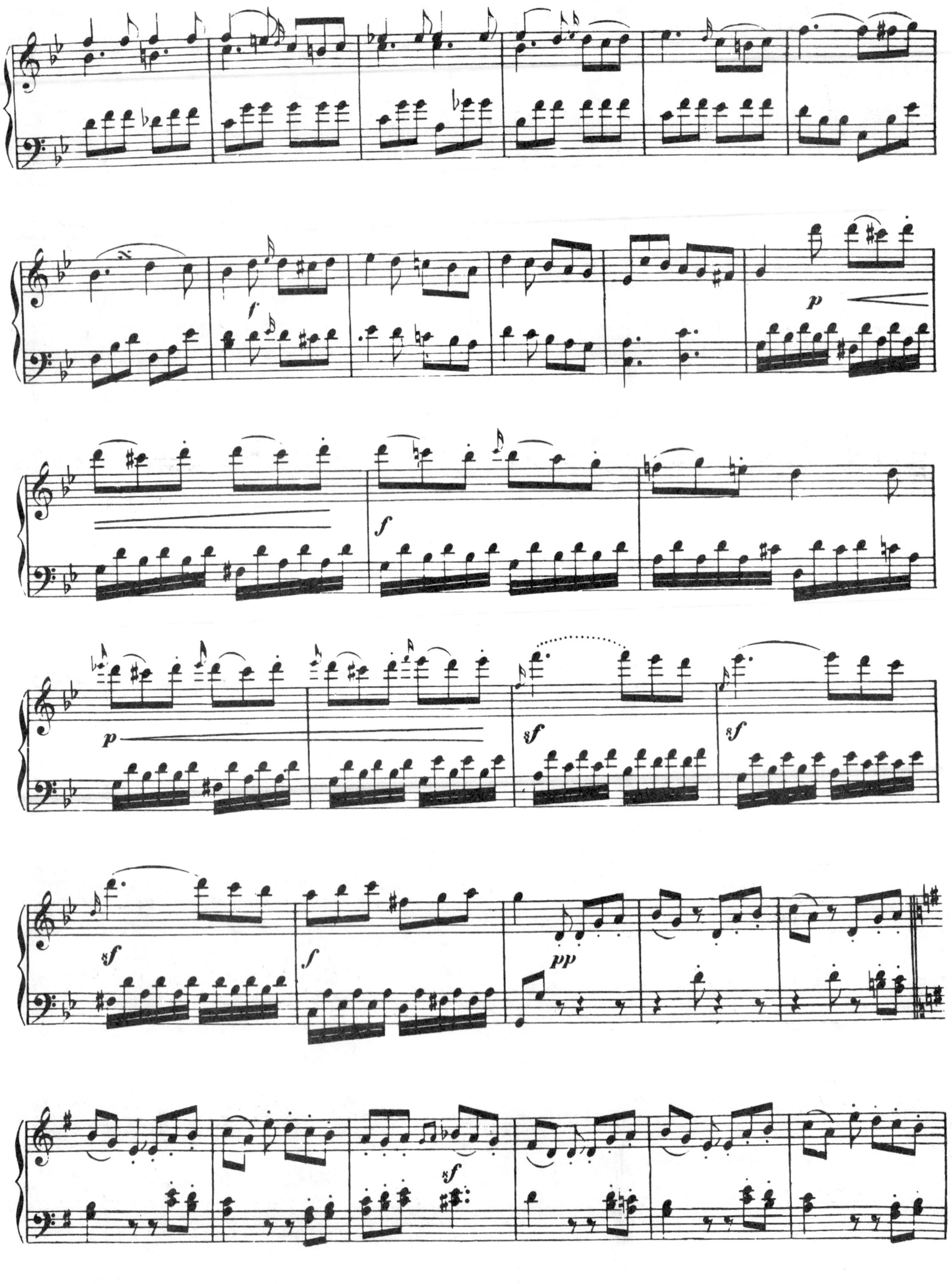

113

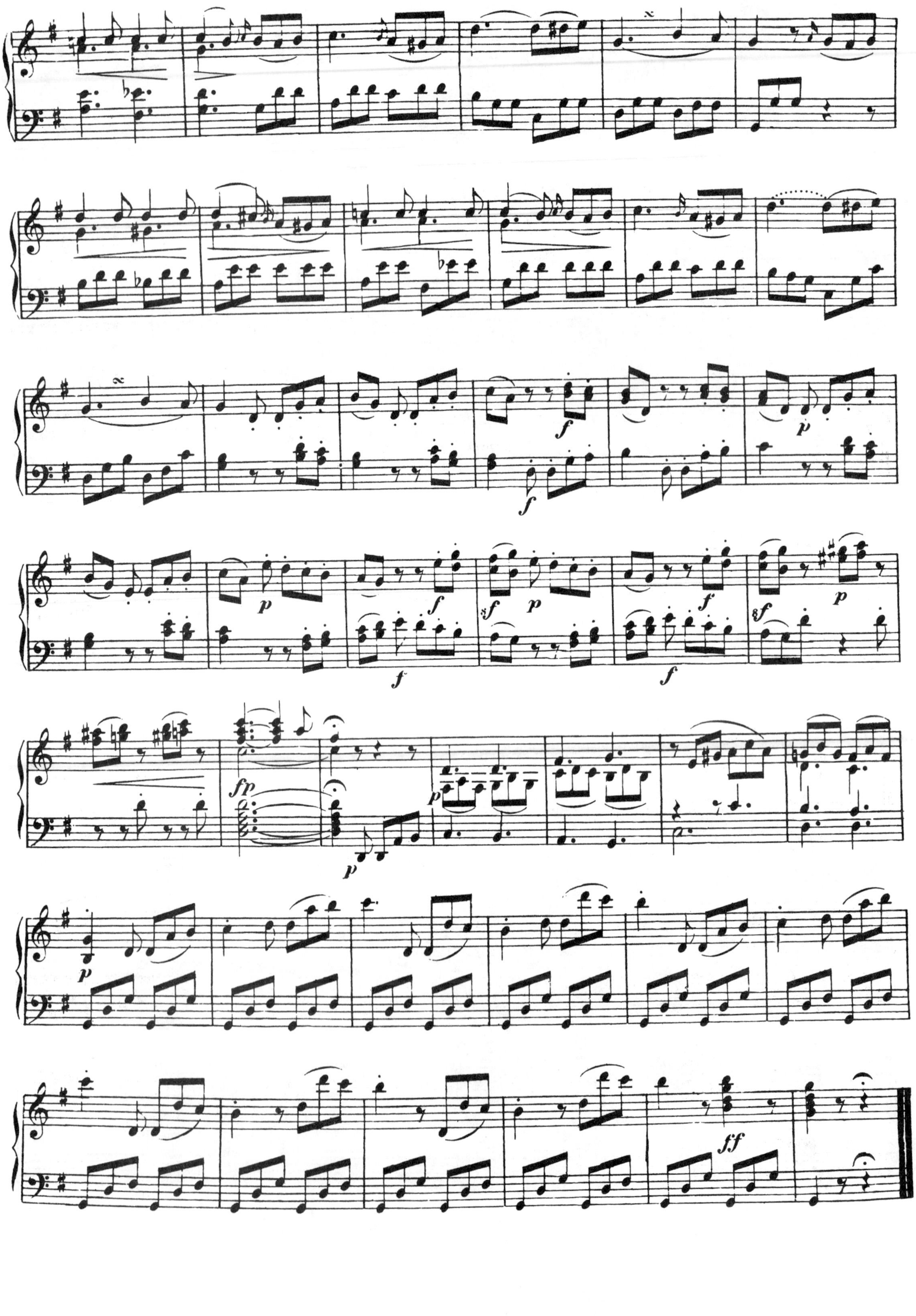

SONATA
Opus 49, No. 2

Allegro ma non troppo

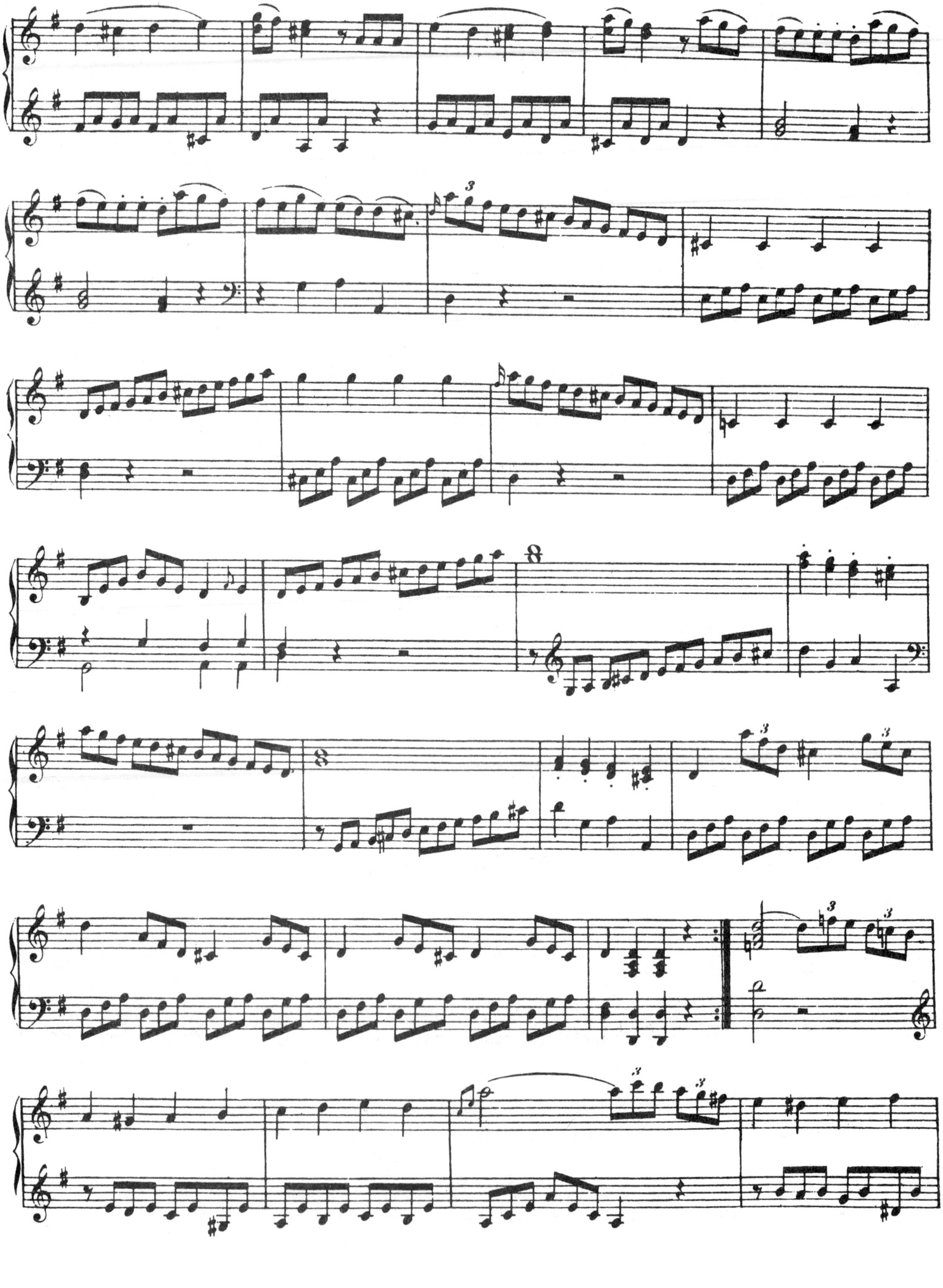

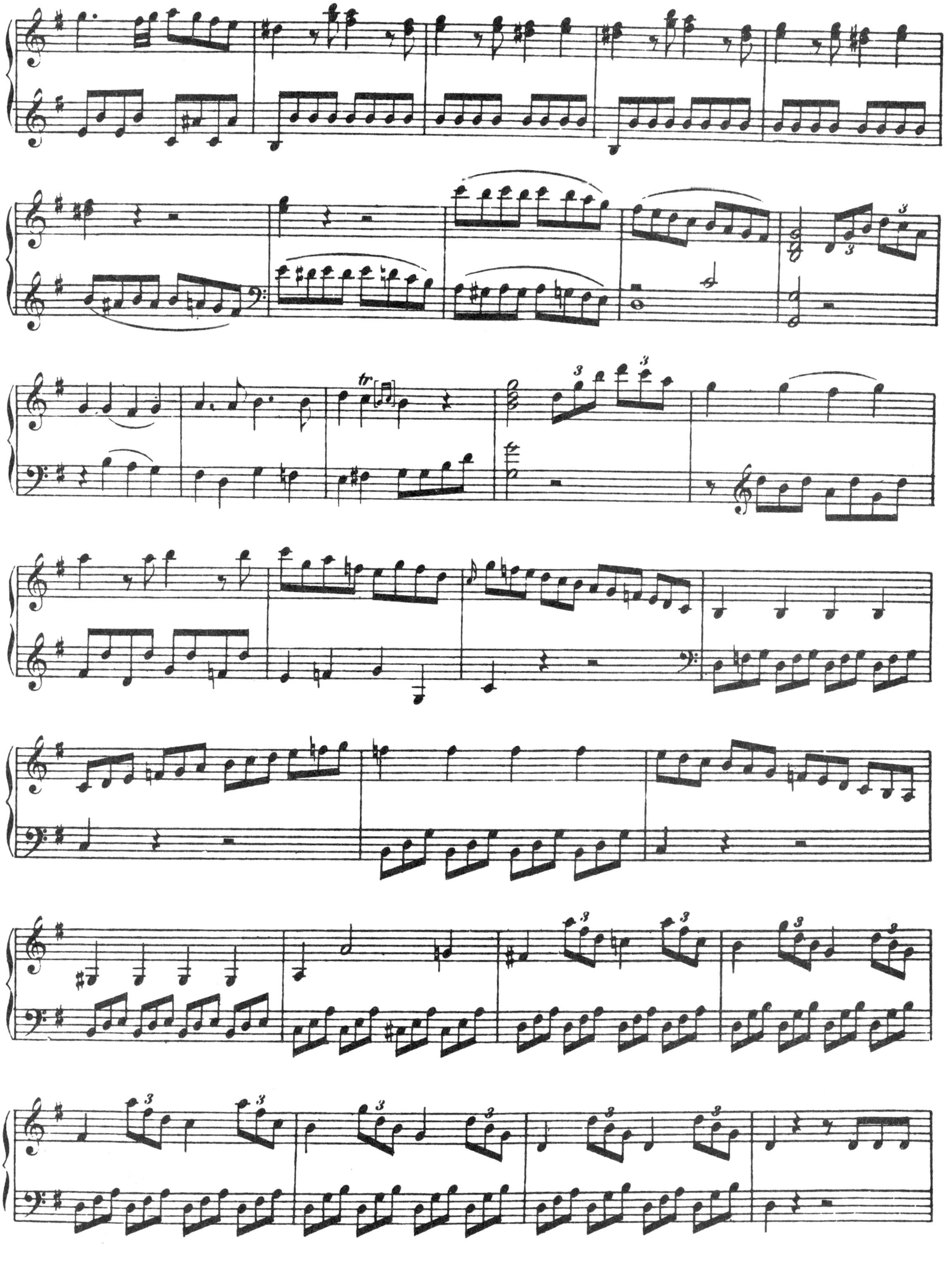
tr
3

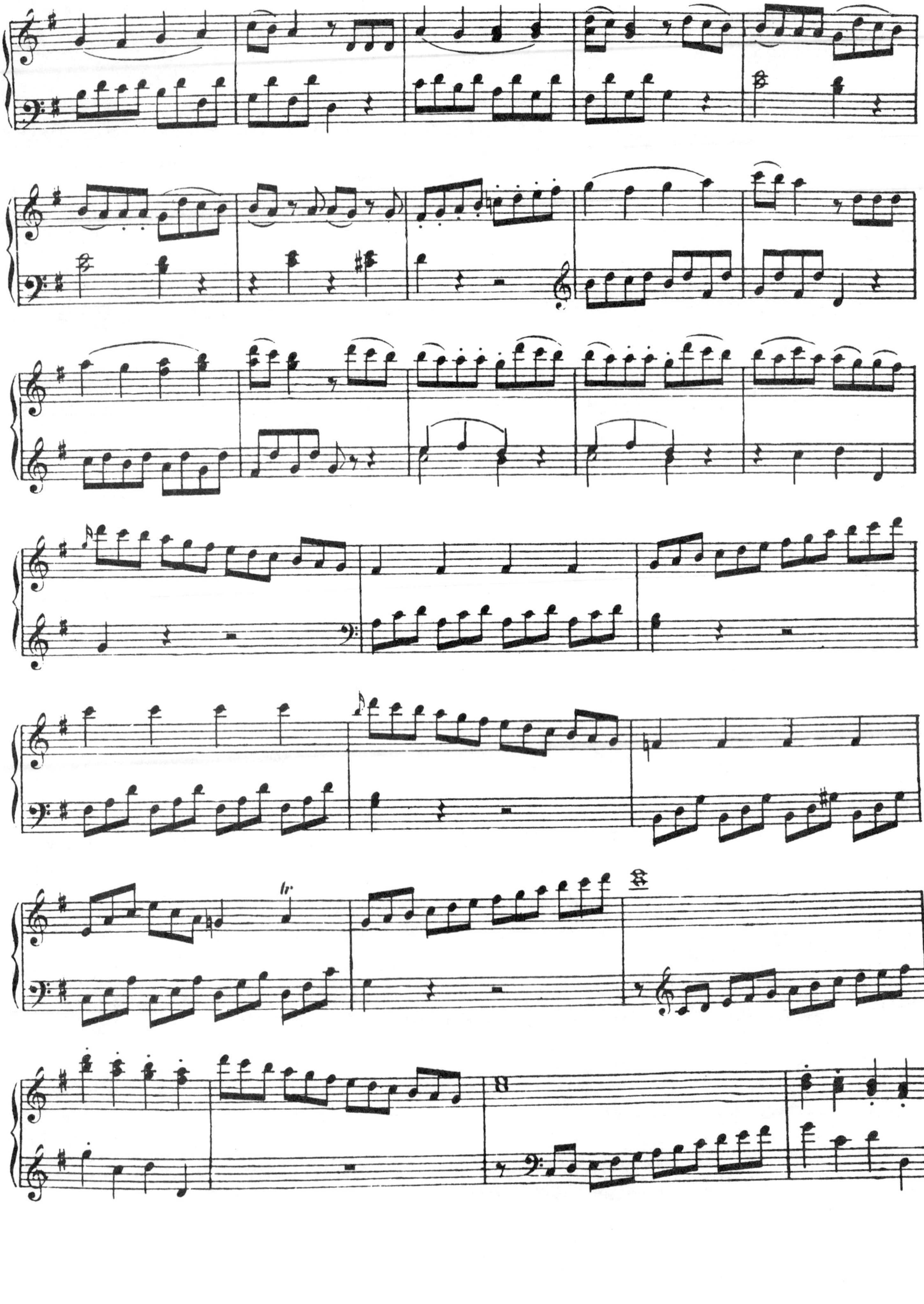
tr

Tempo di Menuetto

120

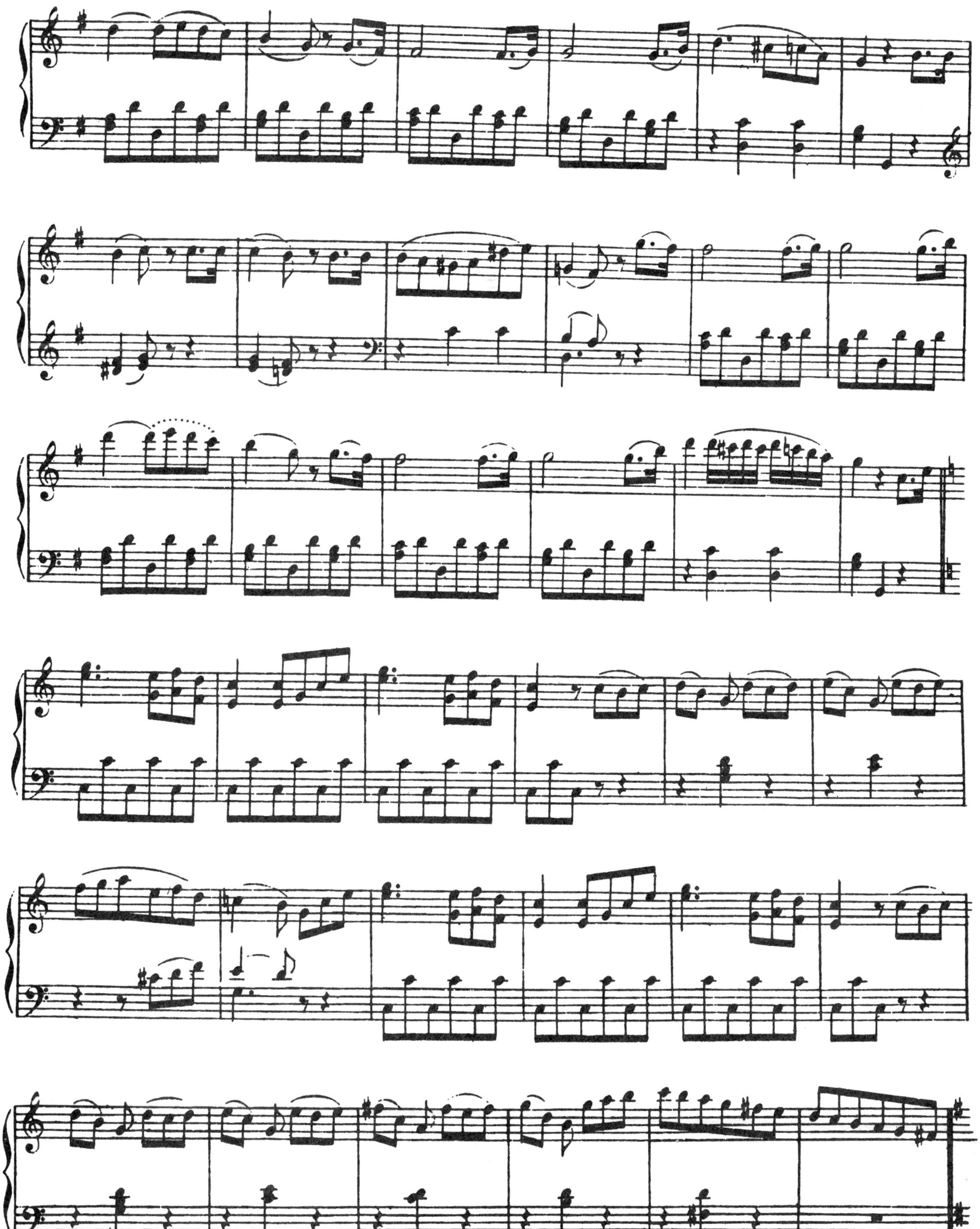

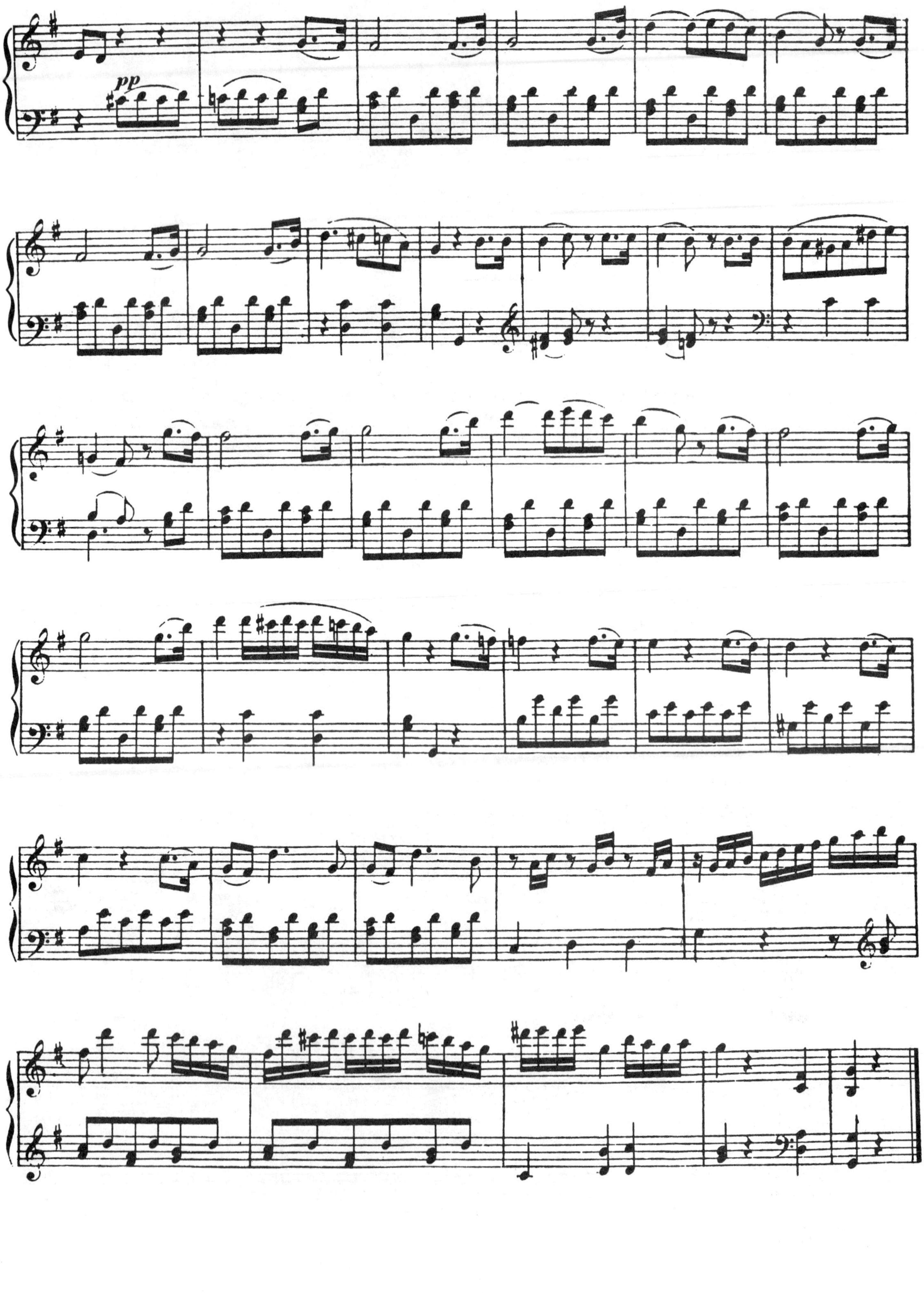
pp

RONDO
Opus 51, No. 1

Moderato e grazioso

p
sf
sf
cresc.
f
p
sempre legato
cresc.
decresc.
p
cresc.
sfp
sf
decresc.
pp
ten.
f

125

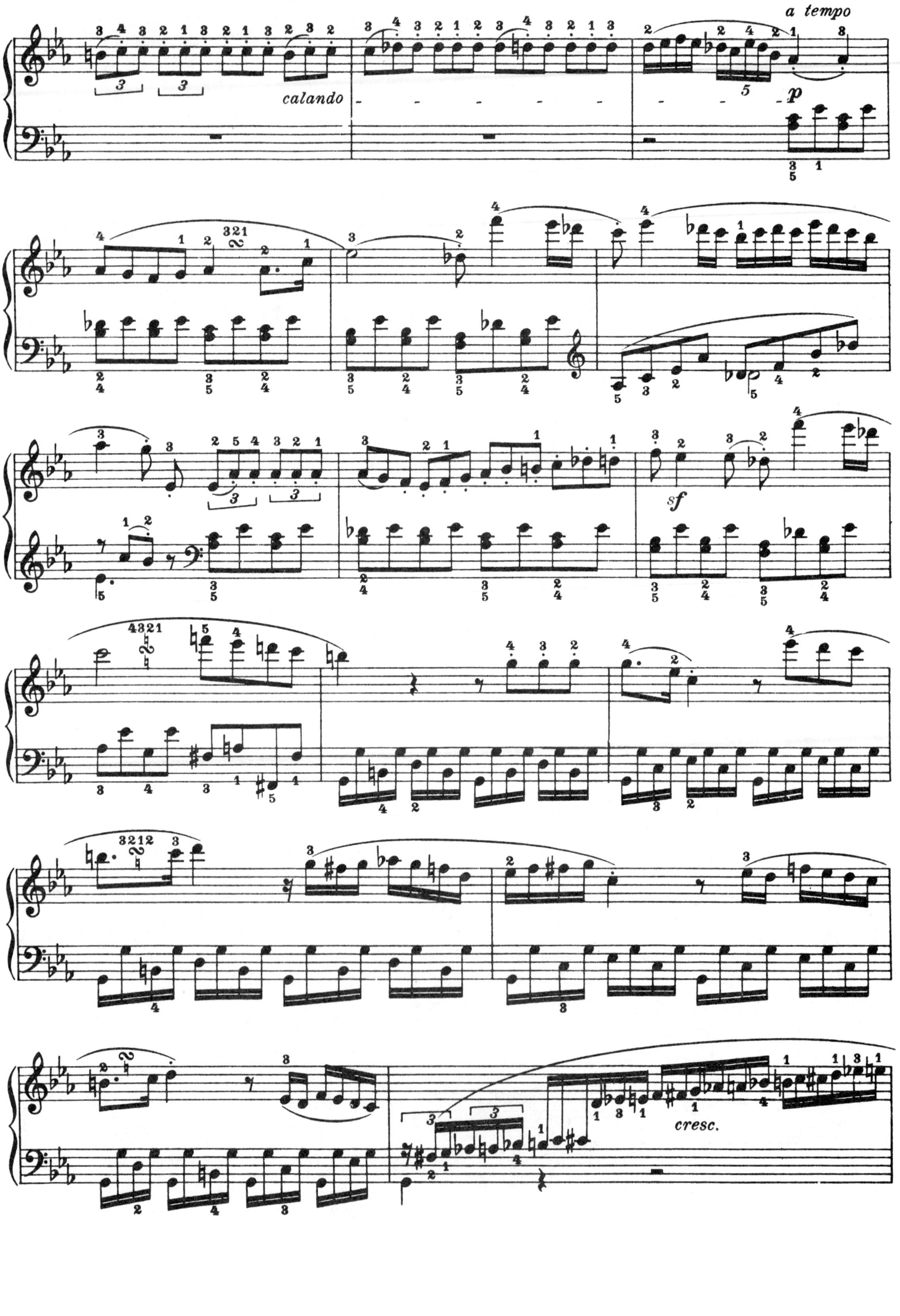
a tempo
calando
p
sf
cresc.

127

128

p ri - tar - dan - do *pp*

cresc.

f

sfp *f*

129

BAGATELLE
Opus 33, No. 2

SCHERZO
Allegro

Minore.

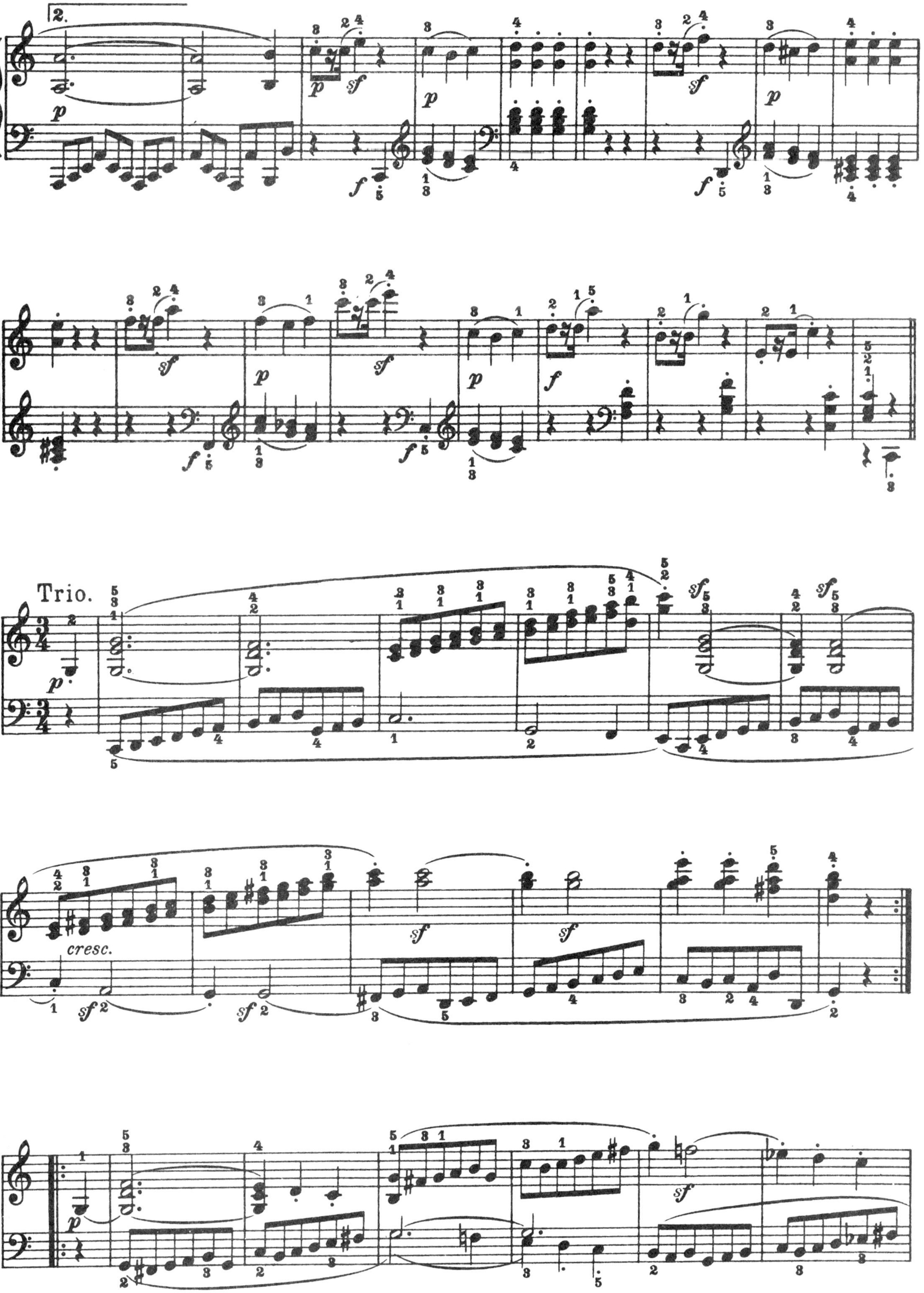
Trio.
cresc.

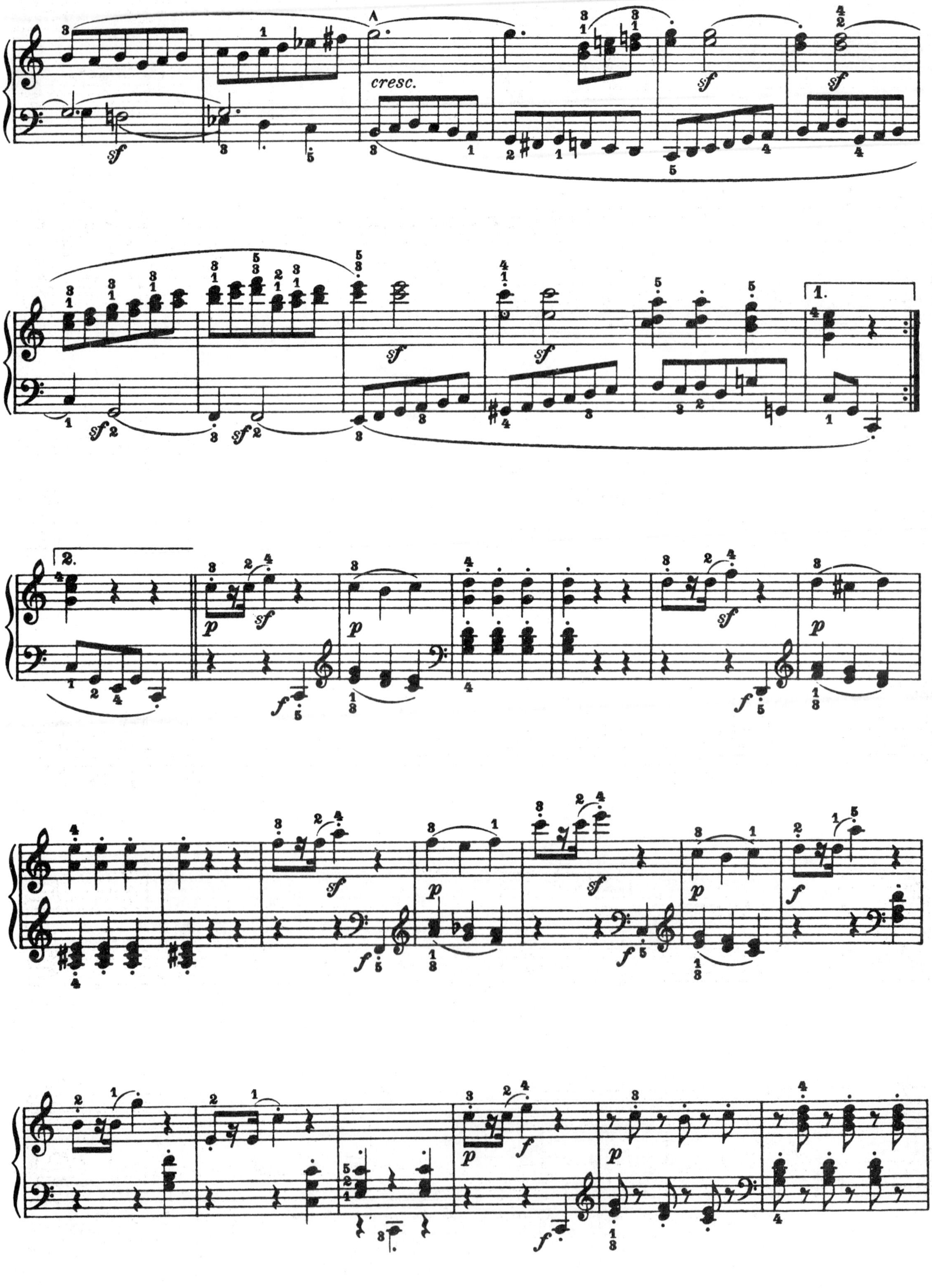
cresc.
1.
2.

133

BAGATELLE
Opus 33, No. 3

Allegretto.

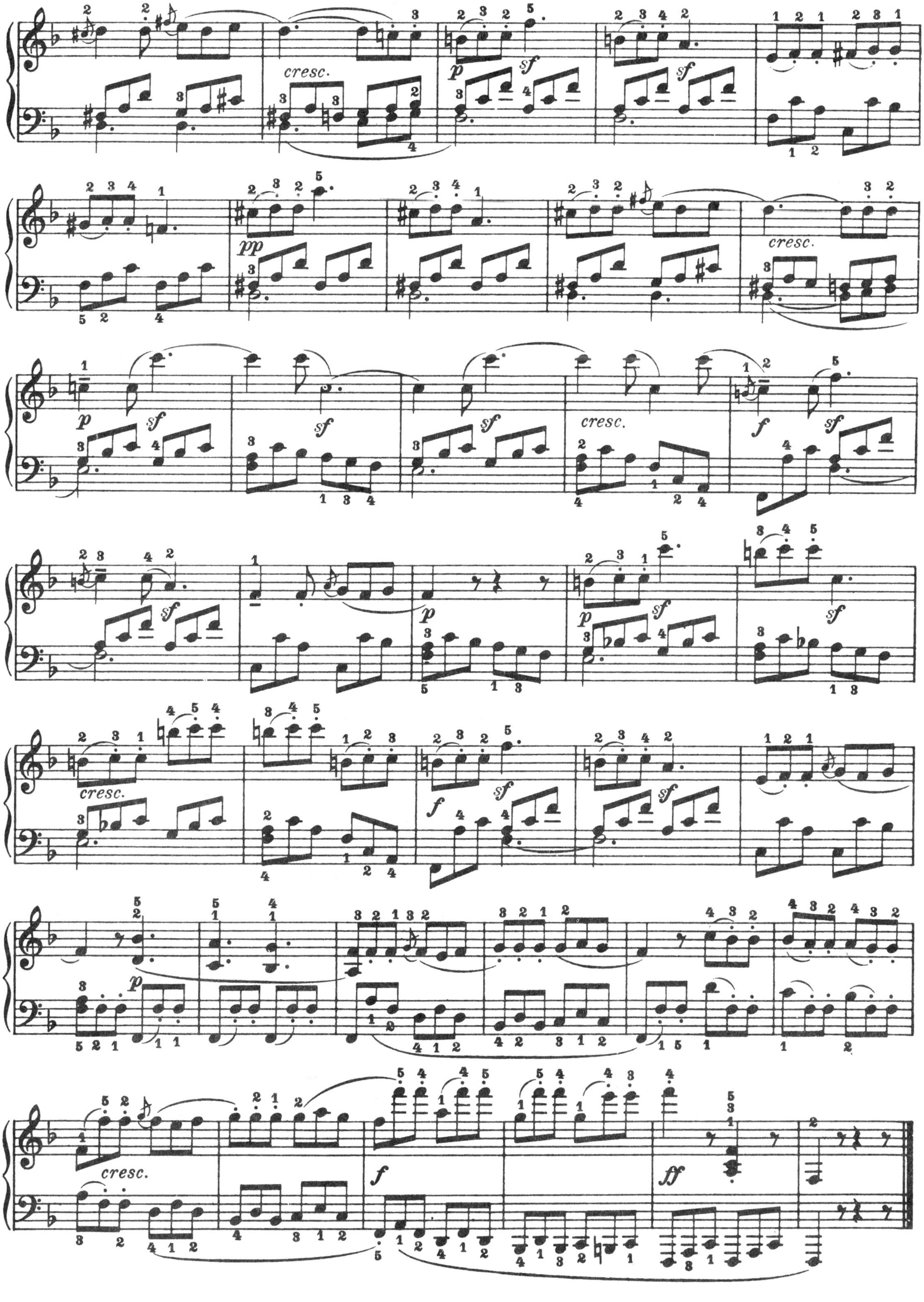
cresc.
cresc.
cresc.
cresc.
cresc.

BAGATELLE
Opus 33, No. 6

Allegretto, quasi Andante
Con una certa espressione parlant

BAGATELLE
Opus 33, No. 7

138

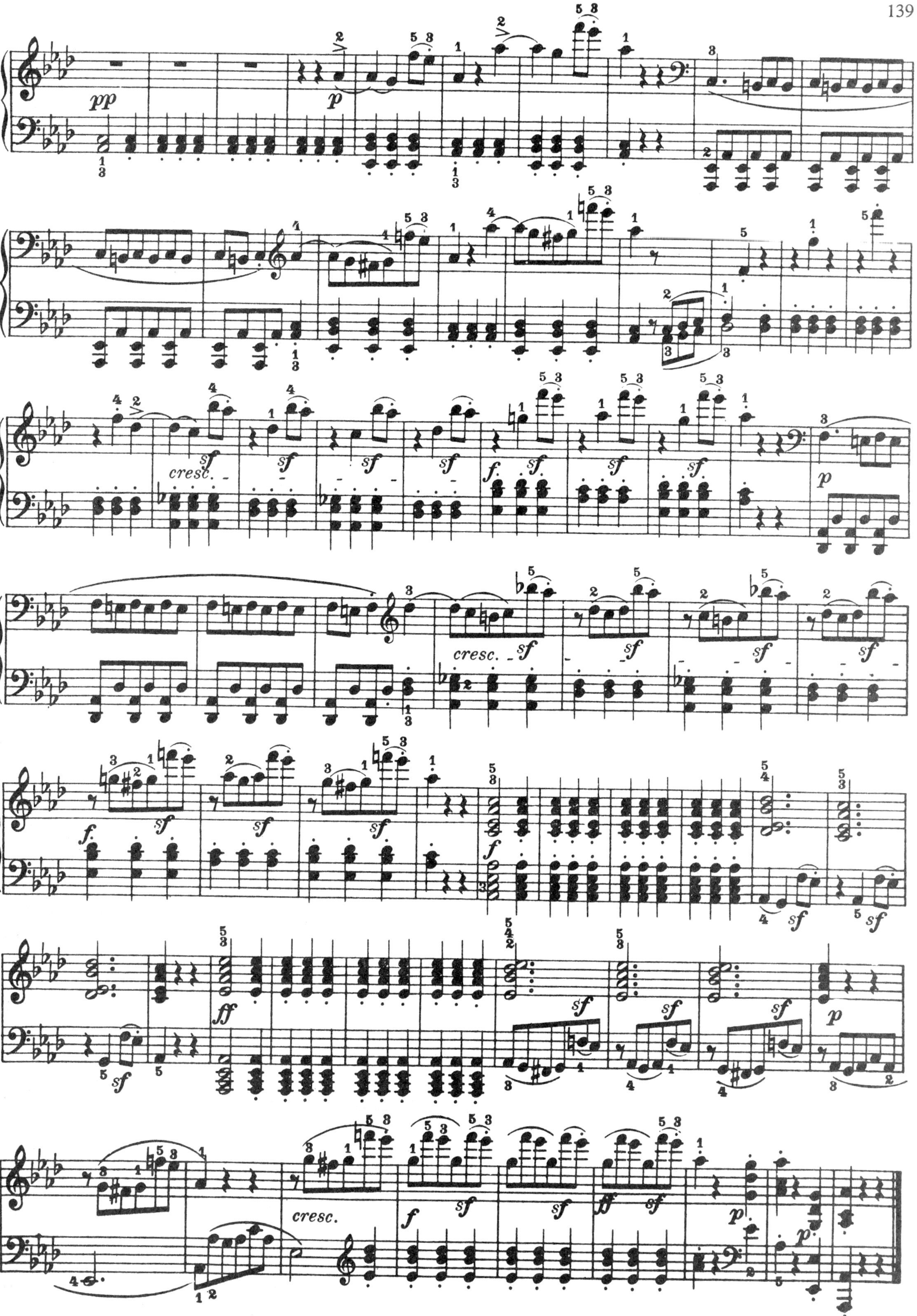
pp
p
cresc.
sf
f
p
cresc.
sf
f
sf
f
sf
sf
ff
sf
p
cresc.
f
sf
ff
p

BAGATELLE
Opus 119, No. 1

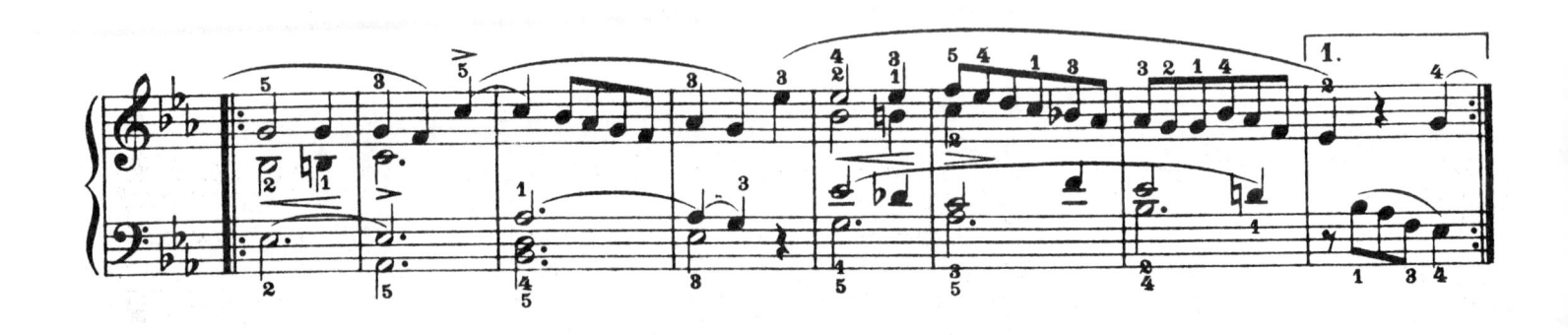

Allegretto

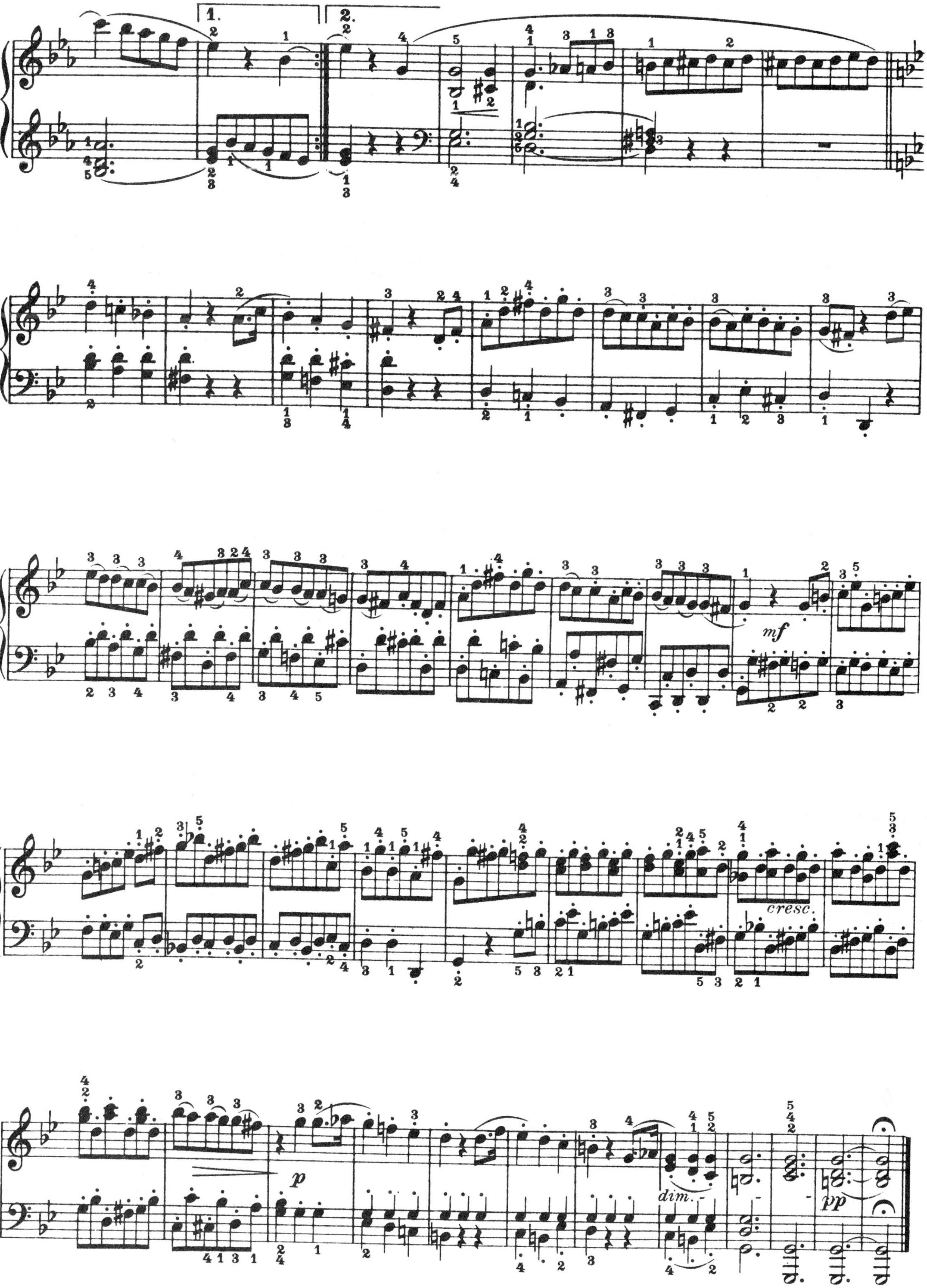
1.
2.
mf
cresc.
p
dim.
pp

BAGATELLES
Opus 119, No. 5

BAGATELLES
Opus 119, Nos. 8 & 9

BAGATELLE
Opus 126, No. 2

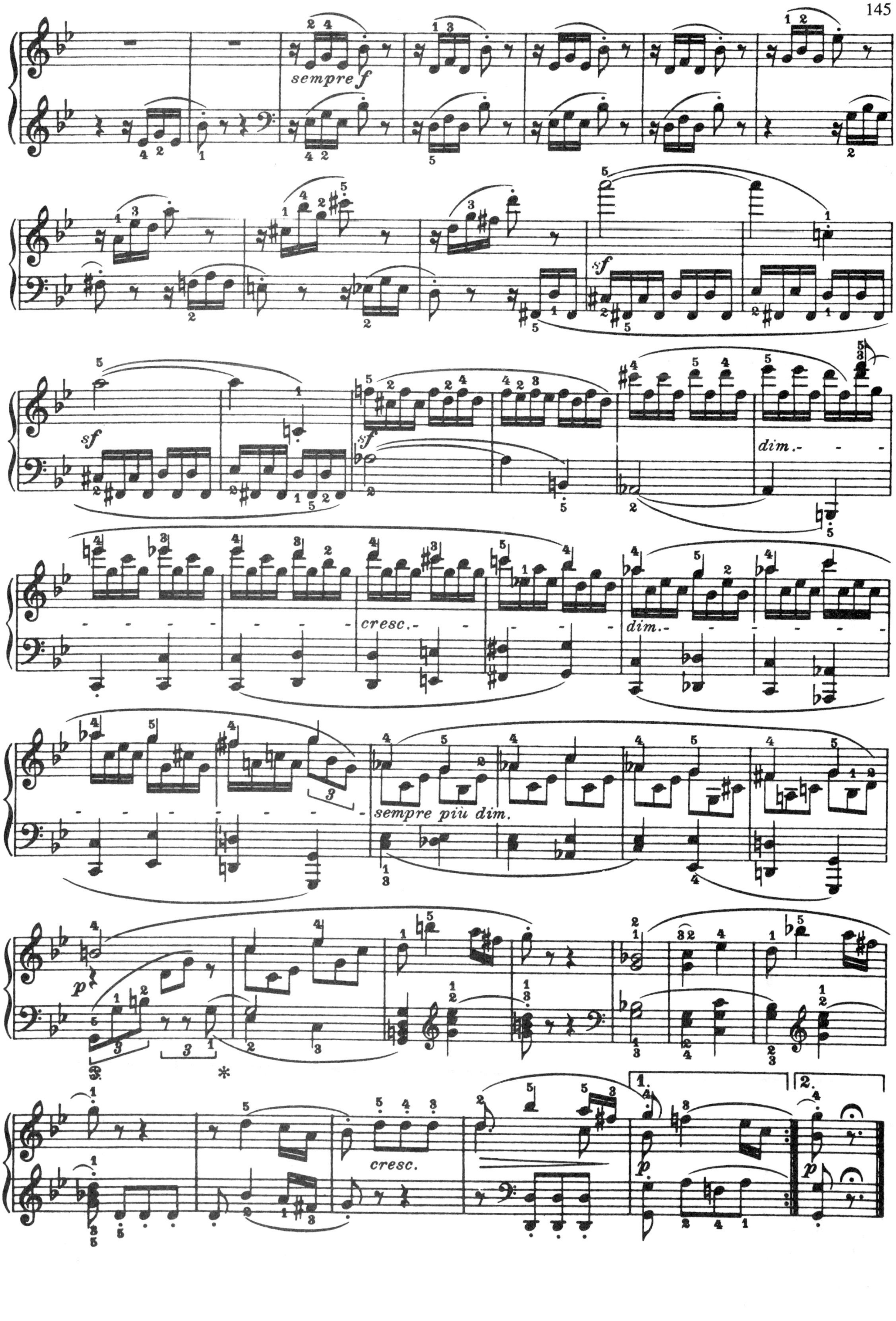
sempre f
sf
sf
sf
dim.
cresc.
dim.
sempre piu dim.
p
cresc.
p
p

RONDO A CAPRICCIO
Opus 129

Allegro vivace

147

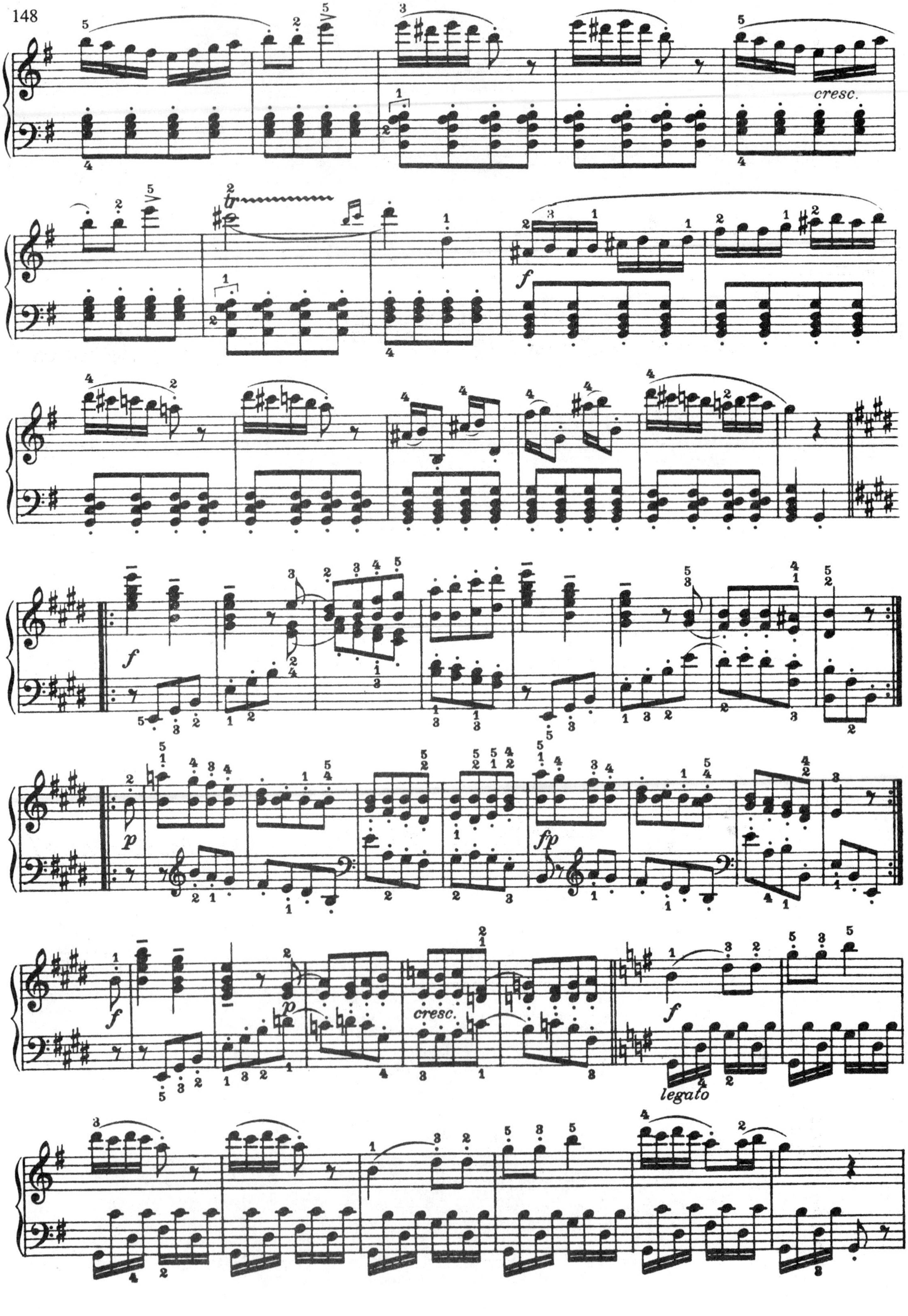
cresc.
tr
f
p
fp
cresc.
legato

149

150

151

152

153

154

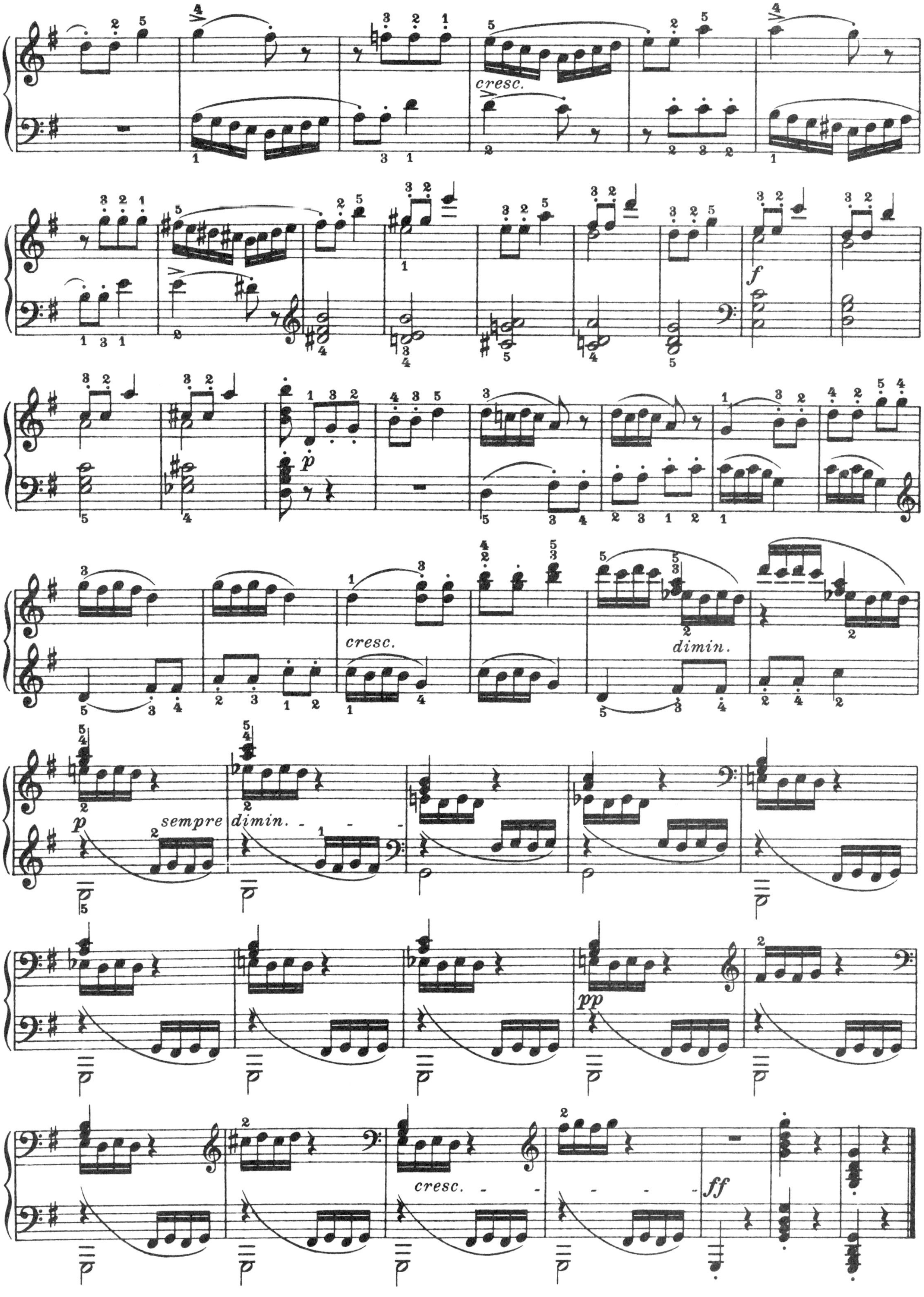
cresc.
f
p
cresc.
dimin.
p
sempre dimin.
pp
cresc.
ff

To Elisabeth Alexiewna, Empress of Russia

POLONAISE
Opus 89

157

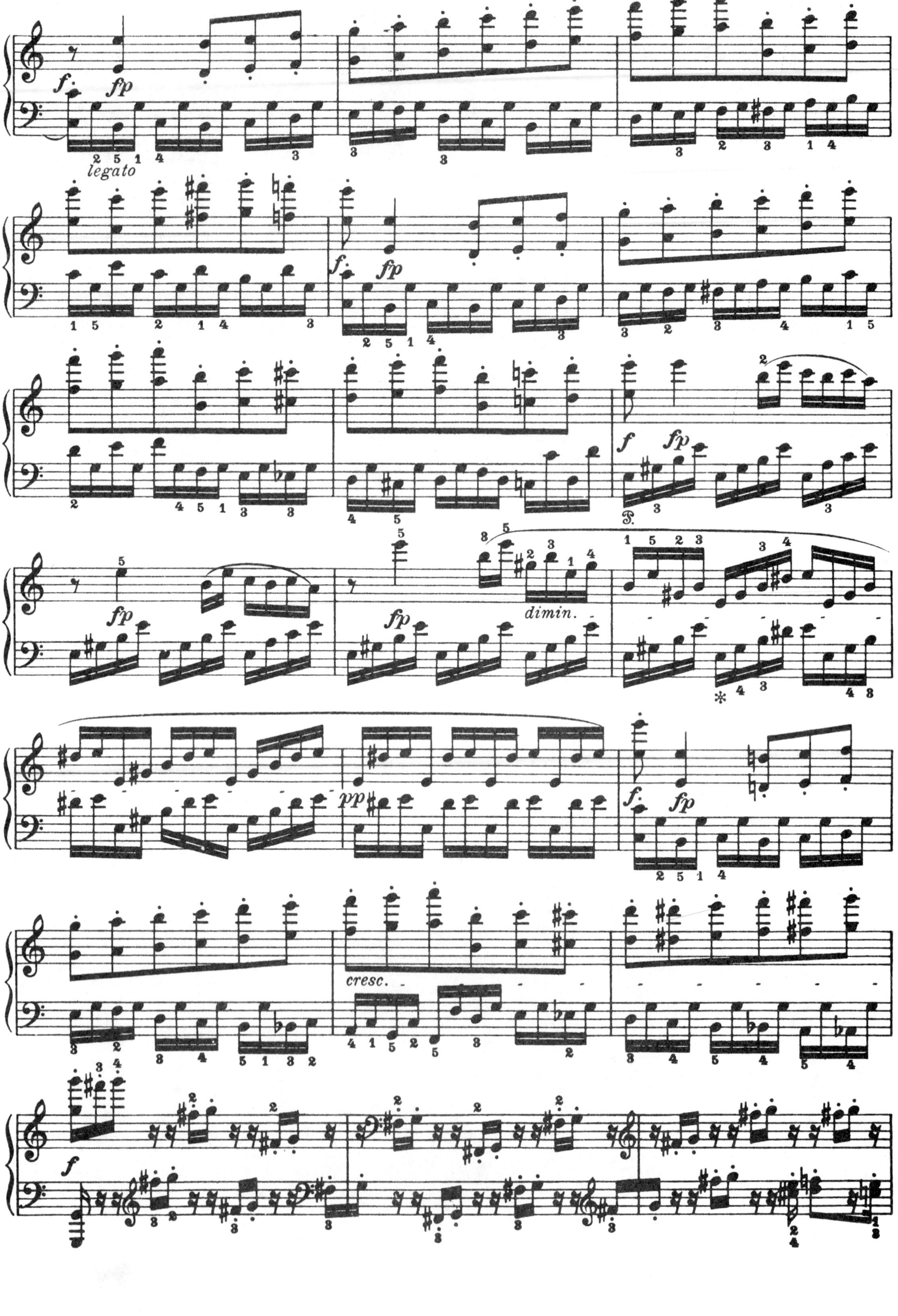
legato
dimin.
cresc.

159

legato
cresc.
dim.
p
dolce
cresc.
p
cresc.
dim.
poco ritard.
a tempo
tr
cresc.

161

162

Poco adagio.

Il tempo primo.

NINE VARIATIONS
on a March by Dressler

Var. II.

Var. III.

165

Var. IV.

Var. V.

167

Var. VIII.

Var. IX. Allegro
f brillante

169

SIX EASY VARIATIONS
on a Swiss song

Maggiore.
Var. IV.
f
sempre legato
mf
p
Var. V.
sempre dolce
pp
Var. VI.
ff
Coda.
tr

SIX VARIATIONS
Opus 76

sf
sf
sf
sf
sf
sf
sf
p
Var. III.
sempre dolce
1.
2.
dolce
1.
2.
Var. IV.
p
leggiermente
p
cresc.
f
p

174

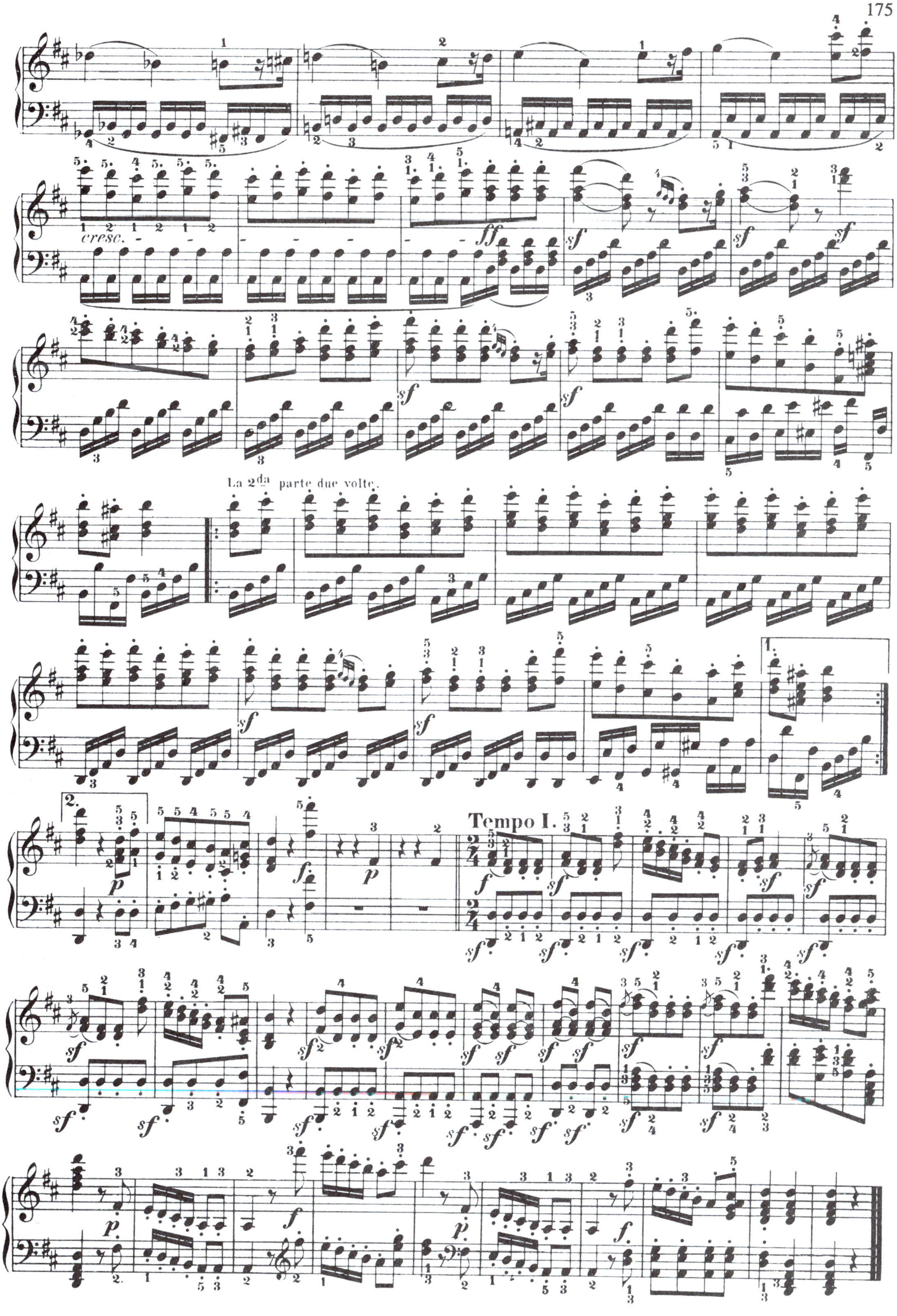
cresc.
La 2da parte due volte.
Tempo I.

SEVEN VARIATIONS
on "God Save the King"

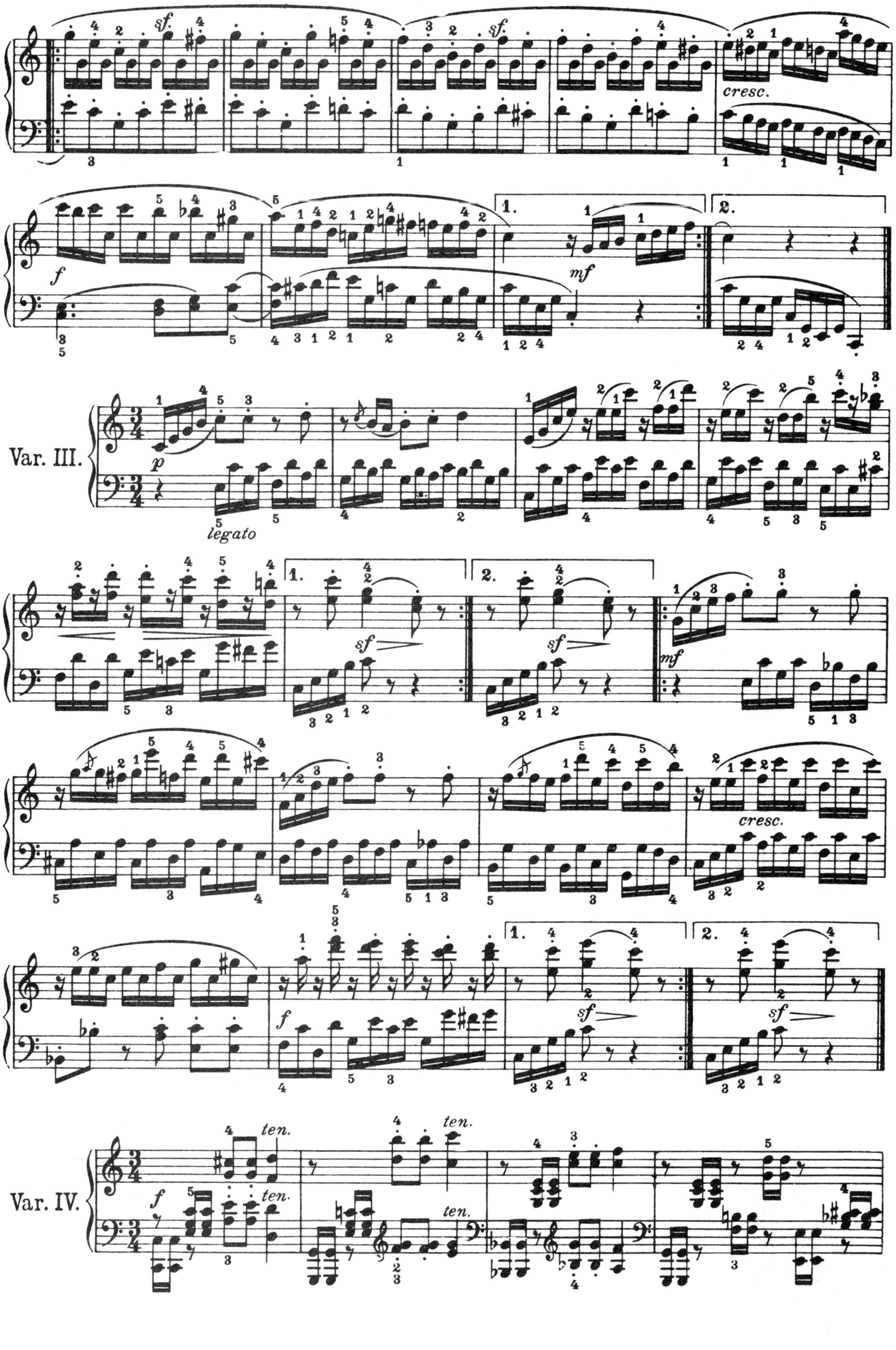
sf.
cresc.
f
mf
Var. III.
p
legato
sf
cresc.
Var. IV.
f
ten.

Var. V. **Con espressione.**

Allegro. Alla Marcia
Var. VI.
p
cresc.
dimin.
1.
2.
p
mf
p
mf
cresc.
f
1.
mf
2.
dimin.
Var. VII.
legato
p
ten.
ten.
mf

180

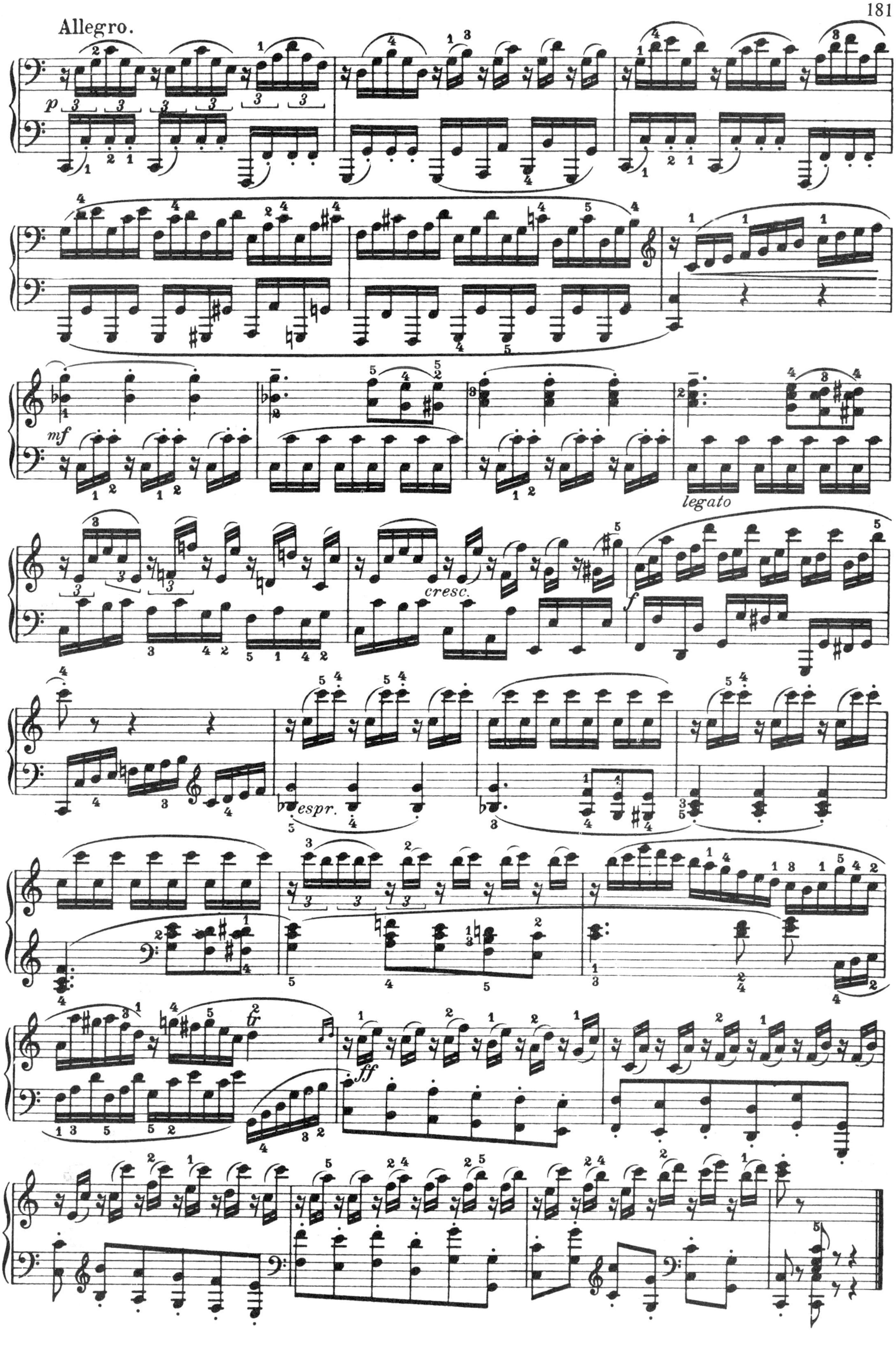
Allegro.
p
mf
legato
cresc.
f
espr.
ff
tr

Selected
DIABELLI VARIATIONS
Opus 120

Poco allegro
Var. II.
p leggiermente
1.
2.
L'istesso tempo
Var. III.
dolce
cresc.
p

Var. IV. **Un poco più vivace**

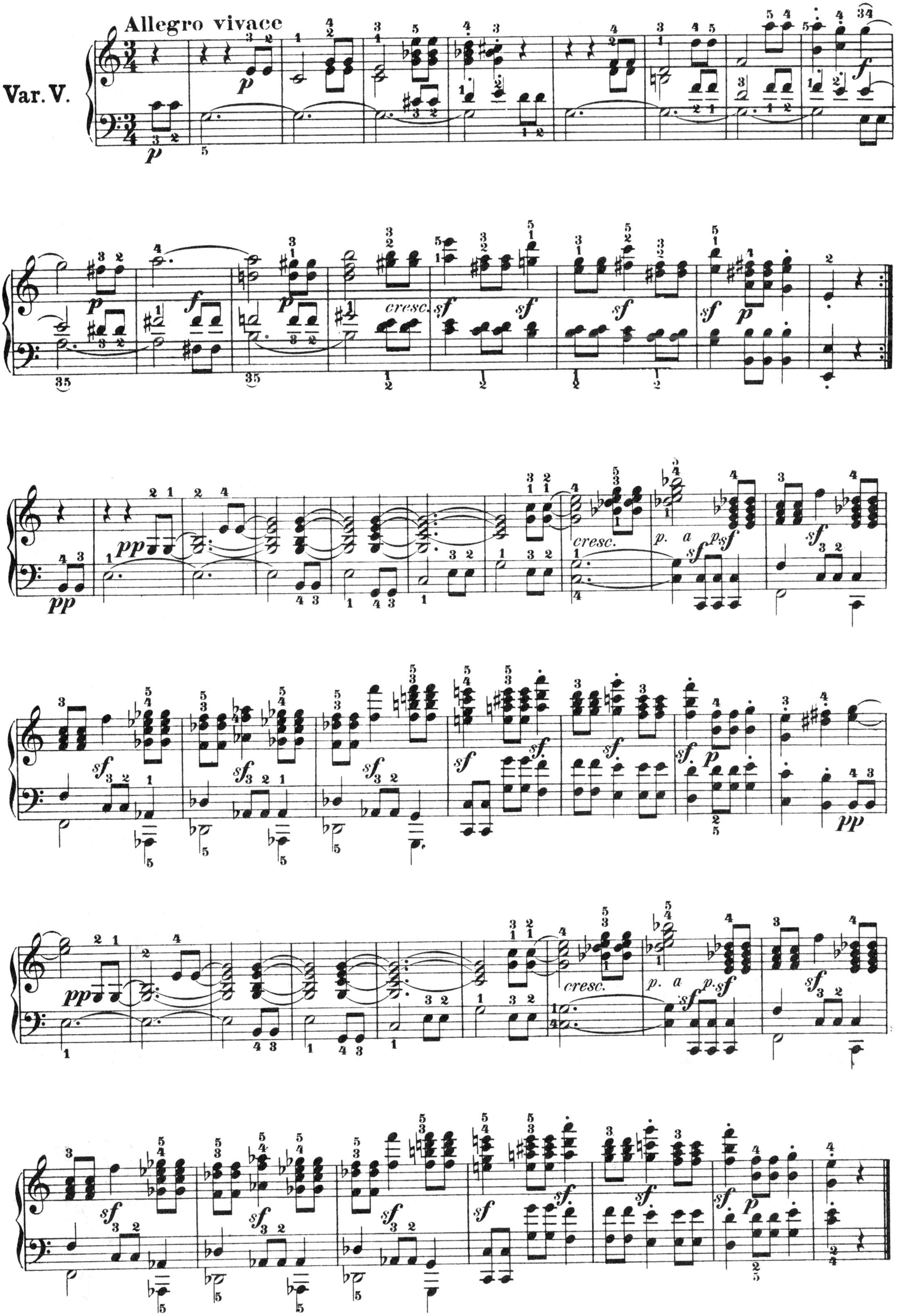
Allegro vivace
Var. V.
cresc.
p. a p.

Var. VII.

Un poco più allegro

Allegro pesante e risoluto
Var. IX.
f
f
sf
sf
sf
sf
sf
p
p
f
p
p
pp
cresc.
f
sf
sf
sf
ff
Presto
Var. X.
pp
sempre staccato
ma leggiermente

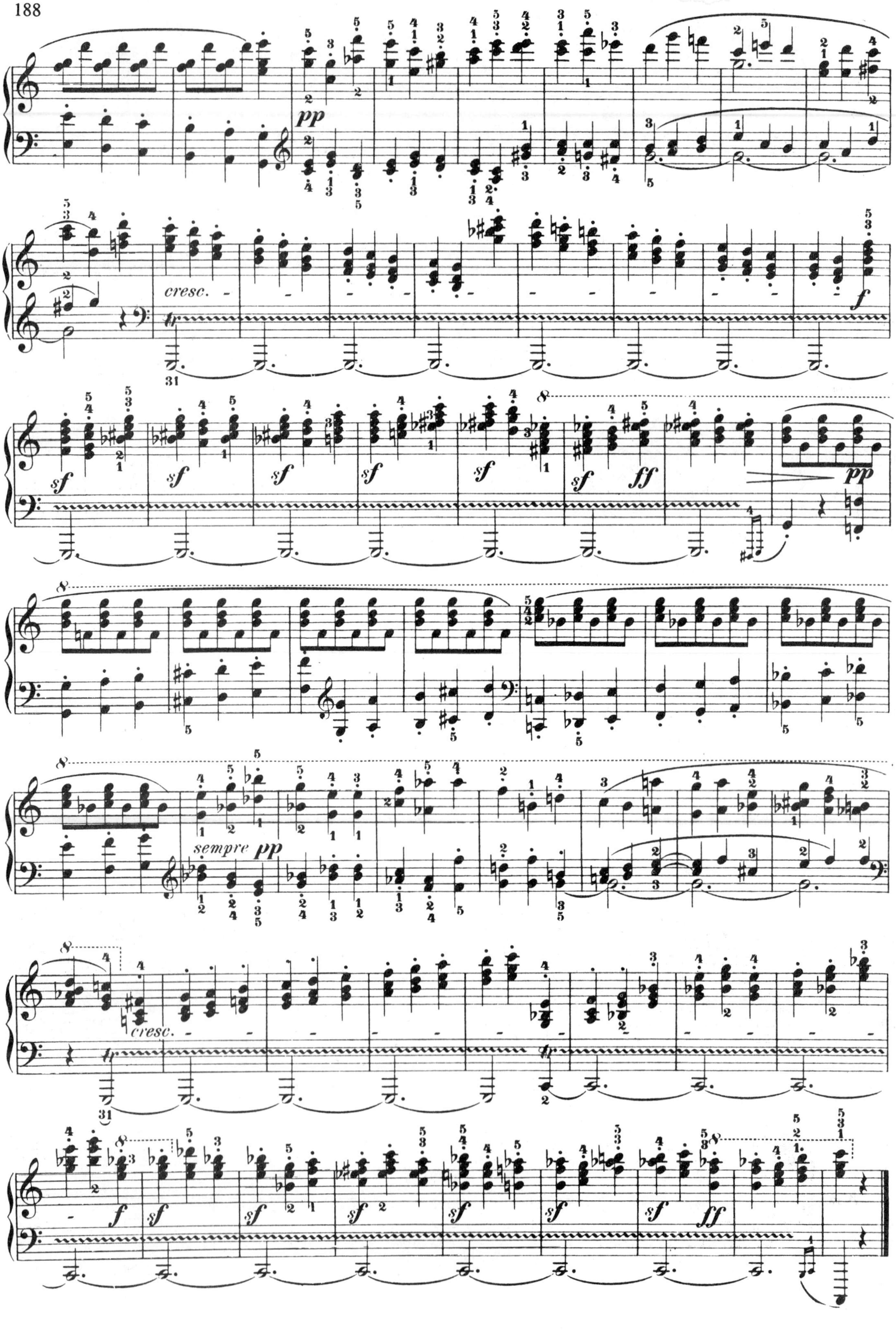
pp
cresc.
f
sf
ff
pp
sempre pp
cresc.
f
sf
ff

189

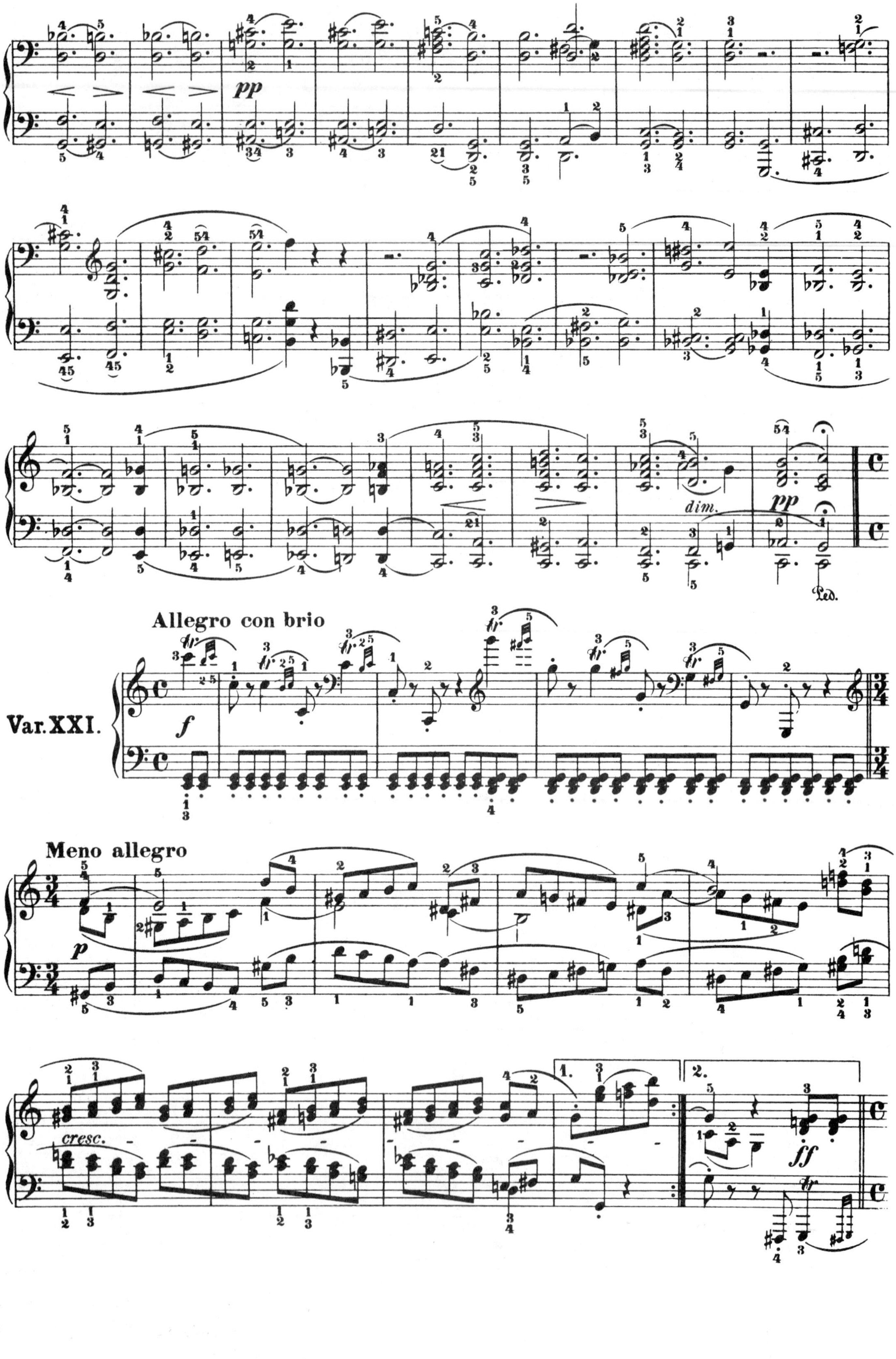
pp
dim.
pp
Allegro con brio
Var. XXI.
f
Meno allegro
p
cresc.
ff

Tempo I
Meno allegro
p
cresc.
p
ff
p
Molto allegro
Alla „Notte e giorno faticar" di Mozart.
Var. XXII.
p
f
p
f
p
cresc.
f
pp
pp
cresc.
al f
più f
ff
p

Allegro
Var. XXV.
p tutte le corde
leggiermente
cresc.
diminuendo
1.
2.
p
cresc.
più cresc.
f
p
1.
2.